nothing
to fear

nothing to fear

The Key to Cancer Survival

Larry Burkett

MOODY PUBLISHERS
CHICAGO

Scripture quotations are taken from the *New American Standard Bible®* [updated], Copyright © The Lockman Foundation 1960, 1962, 1963, 1968, 1971, 1972, 1973, 1975, 1977, 1995. Used by permission.

Edited by Adeline Griffith, Crown Financial Ministries

Library of Congress Cataloging-in-Publication Data

Burkett, Larry.

  Nothing to fear : the key to cancer survival / by Larry Burkett.
      p. cm.
    Includes bibliographical references.
    ISBN 0-8024-1434-6
    1. Burkett, Larry--Health. 2. Kidneys--Cancer--Patients--United States--Biography. 3. Cancer--Alternative treatment. 4. Cancer--Religious aspects. I. Title.

RC280.K5 B873 2003
362.1'9699461'0092--dc21

                                                                2002014330

13 5 7 9 10 8 6 4 2

Printed in the United States of America

Contents

A Word from Judy Burkett . . .

Following a long and courageous battle with cancer and heart disease, my husband Larry Burkett completed his journey of serving our Lord Jesus Christ. God called Larry into His presence at 3 A.M. on July 4th 2003.

My husband was taken home, not as a result of cancer but of heart disease. The principles he used in fighting cancer are timeless and need to be read and applied by many more people.

It was a privilege beyond what I can capture in words to have labored alongside Larry for part of that journey. And I am comforted to know his work will continue through the *Larry Burkett Cancer Research Foundation.*

The LARRY BURKETT CANCER RESEARCH FOUNDATION has been founded to raise money for cancer research and the training of doctors, so that new approaches to cancer treatment can become widely available. By contributing to the foundation, you will be helping cancer patients live longer and more productive lives.

Here's how you can help! As a nonprofit organization, which is sustained through your support, the LARRY BURKETT CANCER RESEARCH FOUNDATION receives donations in two ways.

Online Donations: Donate through our secure web-server:
www.cancertech.org

By Mail: To donate by check or money order, please write to:
LARRY BURKETT CANCER RESEARCH FOUNDATION
PO Box 739
Gainesville, Georgia 30503-0100

Introduction

Since I was first diagnosed with cancer in 1995 I have learned more about cancer than I ever wanted to know.

I have learned that cancer strikes both sexes and all ages, races, and types—athletes and couch potatoes. I also have learned that just about everyone knows a person with cancer. I've learned that eating right and exercising definitely help, but they do not prevent many types of cancer. And, I've learned that the single most important factor in cancer survival is *faith*. (Non-believers want to think of this as "a positive mental attitude.")

There are many other important factors in the battle against cancer, as well as in other life-threatening diseases. To help others shorten the learning curve, I'm going to share some of what I've learned over the last seven years. This is, so to speak, a crash course on cancer survival.

I certainly don't pretend to be a cancer expert or health professional, but I do believe I have discovered some essential truths that make long-term survival quite possible for many people. Helen Keller, who spoke from experience, said, "Although the world is full of suffering, it is also full of the overcoming of it."

Bear in mind that no two people are the same—chemically, physically, mentally, or otherwise. There certainly are basic similarities, and we are a lot more alike than different. But no one size fits all, and thus far there is no magic bullet for cancer. You must seek, evaluate, test, and exercise calm judgment in every situation. The Lord Jesus promises us that if we lack wisdom and we ask in faith God will provide it.

"If any of you lacks wisdom, let him ask of God, who gives to all generously and without reproach, and it will be given to him" (James 1:5). That principle never fails.

Thanks for allowing me to share what I've learned. I pray it will help you, your family, or someone you know.

chapter one
What I Have Learned

In March of 1995 I was stunned to learn that I had cancer. The diagnosis was renal cell carcinoma (kidney cancer) that had metastasized (spread through the body) to my left shoulder blade.

The discovery was a shock to me, but it was a shock that started me on a journey I had never planned. And over the past several years I've learned many things that I trust will be helpful to others. That's the purpose of this book, but remember that it is just a guide—not a bible.

It's Your Body

In the final analysis, no medical doctor is really responsible for your health; *you* are responsible for your health. Doctors may help guide, give alternatives, advise, and administer whatever therapy you choose, but it's *your* body, and you must make the final decisions. If you forget that you're the one responsible for your own health, you can be overrun by the medical system very quickly.

The health care field has many good doctors, but you need to be aware that everyone who graduates from medical school gets an M.D. degree—those who were *first* in their class and also those who were *last* in their class. There are doctors who help and care about their patients, but there also are doctors whose patients represent little more than a day's work. I know, because I've met both kinds.

I personally flee from doctors who don't exhibit empathy for their patients. You must understand that doctors today are involved in one of the biggest and most lucrative businesses in the world. To make a profit, they are required to run their practices as businesses. To do that, doctors have to process a certain number of patients through their offices every day.

You may wait in the doctor's office for two hours or longer, but you are fortunate if you can get 15 minutes of face-to-face communication with your doctor. He or she can't get a lot of information from you in 15 minutes, so your diagnosis and treatment are based on the norms. If you fit within the norms, you're in good shape. If not, you'll need to look elsewhere—quickly.

When you are initially diagnosed with a disease, such as cancer, you probably will be in contact with some high-caliber diagnosticians. These are the specialists other doctors call in when they want to know if you fit the norms.

Because of the use of machines—such as CT scans, MRIs, PET scans, and many other high-tech diagnostic tools—patients tend to think that once that high-caliber diagnosis has been made they'll get the same caliber of help for their cancer at the next level down. That isn't necessarily true.

After you have been given an *accurate* diagnosis, you need to learn as much as you can about your disease as quickly as you can. My diagnosis was metastatic renal cell carcinoma, which is medical jargon for kidney cancer that has spread from one place to another.

I went to the Internet and found that the survival rate for my kind of cancer was very, very low when treated with traditional therapy, because there was no effective treatment for it at that time.

First Discovery

As I said, I learned that the best option for me was probably surgery. Two areas were affected, one in my kidney and one in my scapula (shoulder blade), so the next step was to find the very best surgeons available.

I was helped through a doctor friend at Emory University Hospital in Atlanta, Georgia, where my diagnosis had been made. The really competent doctors usually know all the other competent doctors, so I called and asked, "If you had to have your kidney removed, who would you want to do it?" He gave me the name of the best urological oncologist he knew.

From experience, I've discovered that if you are going to learn anything helpful you must be aggressive in your search. If you're passive, you'll be given directions, not information. In my case, if I'd been passive I might have been shuffled off to the first available surgeon who would have scheduled me to have my kidney removed. Of course, he might have been the best person to do the surgery, but then he might not have been. And I wouldn't have known if I hadn't been searching for the best.

I've found that with cancer, as with most other things, it doesn't take a lot of information to look knowledgeable. I've been researching cancer for less than a decade and only as an interested layperson. Nevertheless, I get calls from people all over the country because they consider me an "expert." That's pretty scary, because I am *not* an expert.

Learn the Language

The next thing anyone who has cancer needs to learn is "doctor language." If you know the language of your disease, a doctor will talk to you. If you don't know the language, he or she will usually talk around you or over you. So learn the language.

Remember the *Honeymooners*, the old Jackie Gleason television show with Art Carney? In one episode Carney's character, Ed Norton, goes to his doctor with a heart problem. The doctor says to him, "I hate to have to tell you this, Ed, but you've had a myocardial infarction."

Obviously relieved, Norton says, "Oh man, that's good, Doc! I thought I'd had a heart attack!" Knowing the language will be in your favor.

I know that there are exceptions to this, but many practicing physicians have limited knowledge about new cancer therapies. They know what they've studied, but if your family doctor graduated 25 years ago or more he or she may have inadequate information about your disease. If your doctor is a competent practitioner, you'll be referred to someone who does know a lot more about your disease than he or she does. If not, your doctor may try to deal with it alone and perhaps limit your chances of survival.

If the cancer is common enough—like ovarian,

prostate, colon, or lung—there's a real risk that your local physician may think he or she is able to handle your problem. Your family physician may be the best doctor to deal with non-life-threatening diseases but probably is not the best to treat cancer. So, if you can afford it, you need to at least consult with a specialist.

Only a small percentage of doctors will think they can handle everything. If your primary physician indicates an unwillingness to get you to the right doctors, you definitely have the wrong doctor.

One Size Doesn't Fit All

Not all cancer treatments will work for everyone. Just because a doctor has successfully used a particular treatment (surgery, radiology, or chemotherapy) on other patients with your disease and some of those patients got well, that doesn't mean if it's used on you that you'll get well. In fact, you may get worse as a result, because every person is different and every treatment is different. So, you need to check out all the treatments that are available (within reason).

Early on, in my case, I had a couple of doctor friends I knew well who weren't at all familiar with my disease, but they did know where to find the information I needed: the Internet. Over the years I've gotten more medical information from the Internet than from anyplace else.

Once I located the best specialist for my disease, I was determined to see him and I contacted his office. I described my problem to his assistant and offered to purchase one hour of the doctor's time. I explained, "I don't expect him to treat me; I just want to find out what I need to know."

The doctor was intrigued by my offer, and I ended up paying him $1,000 to give me one hour of his time. That's a lot of money, but it was the best money I've ever spent. He pointed me in the right direction and saved me hundreds of hours of research.

Because this doctor was a researcher and had looked into virtually everything available, I was able to learn exactly what my disease was, what it was prone to do, and what treatments were available—both traditional and nontraditional.

The first question I asked him was, "If your son had the cancer I have, what would you suggest for him?" He outlined what he thought I should do.

The specialist I sought was in New York City, but the right doctor for you could be anywhere. Over the last several years I've talked to doctors in Helsinki, Amsterdam, Paris, Jackson, and Atlanta. You must be aggressive about your own research in order to learn what you need to know.

Treatments Can Be Dangerous

Another thing I've learned is that some traditional cancer treatments are, in fact, very dangerous.

For example, most chemotherapies are systemic poisons. A percentage of people being treated for cancer die from the chemotherapy, rather than from the cancer itself. Although advances are being made with products known as "targeted chemotherapy" for some forms of cancer, most chemicals do not distinguish between diseased and healthy tissues. I'm not suggesting that chemotherapy is not the right treatment for your disease, but you need to educate yourself and weigh the choices very carefully. Remember that *you* are responsible for your own health.

I've taken a lot of alternative treatments. When doctors ask if I have clinical data on the results of the alternative treatments, I tell them that U.S. quality studies are not available.

Usually, traditional therapy doctors will then ask how I know an alternative treatment works and what percentage of the people who use it get well. That's a fair question, and often there is only anecdotal data available. The bottom line is that you must trust the doctors involved.

I've found that the data on many traditional treatments is pretty abysmal. With some cancers, a 10 to 15 percent survival rate after chemotherapy is considered acceptable. I don't consider that a one-out-of-ten chance of surviving after treatment is very good. If that's the best available, fine, but I'll look for better odds if possible.

Radiation therapy for cancer is steadily improving, but there are more options than a typical radiologist at a small hospital knows about. There are therapies like the three-dimensional or stereodactic radiation, ultra high-speed radiation, proton beam radiation, and so on. The technology improves almost daily, and there is a large variety of new tools that allow the patients to receive minimal unnecessary exposure to radiation.

Your doctor may or may not know about these diagnostic tools. All physicians have to attend regular refresher courses, but you have no way of knowing if your doctor is a slow learner, a sleeper, very attentive, or out to lunch at those seminars. So it's important to research whether there are other options available.

Some Alternatives Do Work

Not every alternative therapy is a sham. The tendency in traditional medicine is to think that if it's not FDA-approved, it's worthless. That simply is not true.

The medical standards we have set in this country are costly in both time and money. Typically, it can cost tens of millions to hundreds of millions of dollars to get a new therapy or drug through our FDA approval process.

In addition, the process often takes several years and all too often involves double-blind studies: to obtain comparison data, a ratio of patients are given placebos. Many physicians and patients (myself included) find this unconscionable. Only companies with access to huge amounts of capital can pay the price of FDA clinical studies.

Many companies in other countries either cannot or will not pay that price, including most Asian and European countries. That does not necessarily mean that the medicine they practice is second rate, and it doesn't mean that the therapies they're using are worthless. Generally, we would call most of their methods and therapies *alternatives*.

I investigate alternative therapies all the time. When I discover a therapy that I think may be beneficial to me, I set criteria before I consider using it. I will discuss those more fully in Chapter 5.

There are new therapies—vaccines, stem cell transplants, and so forth—that may be better than traditional therapies, such as chemotherapy. You owe it to yourself and your family to investigate.

The cancer death rate in our country is going down, but it is not because we have better cancer therapies; it's because we have better diagnostic tools that detect cancer at earlier stages, when it is easier to cure.

New therapies like vaccines and genetic modifications are under study, but they're not available to the vast majority of patients. Some of these new tools are in clinical studies that may take years or decades to complete. In the meantime, critically ill cancer patients who might benefit from some of these therapies will die. To me, this makes no sense.

Make It Legal

You can change the "system." It's a sad commentary on our society that in most states a 13-year-old girl can walk into an abortion clinic and get an abortion without her parent's permission, and yet a 65-year-old man cannot get a cancer treatment because it hasn't been FDA approved. Without this approval, most doctors cannot (or will not) recommend the treatment.

The state of Georgia and seven other states have changed the law. Now patients have access to alternative therapies, as long as a licensed physician administers them. For further information about this law, see "Other" in the Appendix.

As I said, it has been my observation that virtually everyone knows someone with cancer, and almost everyone knows someone with a cancer that has been determined untreatable by traditional methods. These patients are considered terminal by medical standards.

That's why we helped to get the law changed in our state. At least there's hope where there was none before. Cancer isn't Democratic or Republican; it's a bipartisan issue. Don't ever presume that you can't change the *status quo*. Passion is the key to getting things done.

The Treatment Must Fit the Patient

I've discovered that, just as not all alternative therapies are worthless, neither are all alternative therapies worthwhile. I meet people all the time who think that alternative treatments are the only way to go and that doctors have some kind of conspiracy with the FDA and pharmaceutical companies to prohibit new cancer cures from being developed. That is nonsense! It is rare to find a doctor who doesn't want to help his or her patients. Most of them may not know as much as they could, but with rare exceptions they do want to help.

It's important for the treatment to blend with your personality. I met an excellent doctor from Helsinki, Finland who said he had developed a very effective treatment for the cancer I have. He sent me his therapy in two large boxes—enough to treat me for three months. After evaluating it, I decided that it was much too complicated for my lifestyle. If I had dedicated myself to this doctor's therapy, I could not have continued to do what God called me to do, and that was unacceptable to me.

Even though he had clinical studies showing that in five years he had never lost a patient with my type of cancer, I passed it up. Why? It required a total life commitment that I was not willing to make.

The same thing can be said of some cancer diets. I have no doubt that many diets help those with cancer. But, to stay on most of these diets, you'd have to travel with a juicing machine; pounds of raw, organic vegetables; and a colonic machine. I decided, *If that's what it takes I can't do it.*

So I search for treatments that blend with my personality and lifestyle. I take good nutritional supplements, avoid most hormone-treated meats, drink ozonated water, and do an IV immune therapy twice a year.

Whatever therapy you decide on must fit *your* personality and *your* lifestyle, and everybody is different. My plan works well for me, but I'm not suggesting that you should follow my plan. I have found it beneficial, but it may not fit you.

If you have to dedicate your whole life to a therapy just to stay alive, you must decide if it's worth it. A 32-year-old mother with three children might be willing to do whatever it takes. But for me—a 64-year-old guy doing radio broadcasts, teaching seminars, writing books, and traveling a lot —it's not worth it.

As I said, I watch my diet, take supplements, and use an IV therapy to try to keep my immune system strong. I can pack everything I need in a small bag that allows me to travel. Consequently, this matches my lifestyle and temperament.

It's Your Life

Remember, it's your life that's on the line. Your family doctor can treat you for colds and the flu, but when it comes to diagnosing and treating cancer you want the best specialist you can find. That's a must!

One of the other things I have found is that cancer tumors are relatively easy to kill. They are tenacious if not treated, especially if they begin to spread, but they can be killed easily if detected early enough.

One invasive radiologist I met has been treating cancer tumors with alcohol for years: he injects the tumors with an alcohol solution that destroys most of them.

Another physician I now have great respect for, Dr. Patrick Sewell at the University of Mississippi Medical College, does the same thing with cryogenics (freezing) or radiofrequency ablation (heat). I will discuss this therapy a little later in the book.

Control Is As Good As a Cure

One thing is for sure: If you live long enough, you're going to die from something. The object isn't necessarily to cure cancer but to control it so it won't kill you. Ignorance, indifference, and passivity will kill you if you ignore the symptoms of cancer.

People rarely have obvious cancer symptoms until very late in the progression of the disease— for example, when it attacks a vital organ. The key is to get regular check-ups and not ignore subtle persistent symptoms.

The Importance of Attitude

Charles Swindoll has said, "I am convinced that life is 10 percent what happens to me and 90 percent how I react to it. And so it is with you."

Your *attitude* is very important. Since no one is going to live forever, what you strive to do is live as long as you can in reasonably good health—without fear. The more you worry, the greater the probability that you will not live as long as you could. Worry affects your spiritual well-being, as well as your immune system and your entire body.

Among my reasons for writing this book was not only to help you in your battle with cancer but to be sure that you understand how I've been able to live without ongoing fear and anxiety.

"[Anxiety] is an emotion that a person experiences in the face of a perceived threat or a danger. . . . [W]hether the danger is real or imagined, the anxiety and all of its symptoms are absolutely real. . . . These feelings can burden the body until insomnia, lack of concentration, pain, and other problems result."[1]

In the New Testament, many encouraging Scriptures explain why we should not worry or be fearful. Unfortunately, even Christians ignore what may be the most well-known cure for anxiety, given by Jesus Christ in Matthew's gospel.

"For this reason I say to you, do not be worried about your life, as to what you will eat or what you will drink; nor for your body, as to what you will put on. Is not life more than food, and the body more than clothing?

"Look at the birds of the air, that they do not sow, nor reap nor gather into barns, and yet your heavenly Father feeds them. Are you not worth much more than they? And who of you by being worried can add a single hour to his life?

"And why are you worried about clothing? Observe how the lilies of the field grow; they do not toil nor do they spin, yet I say to you that not even Solomon in all his glory clothed himself like one of these. But if God so clothes the grass of the field, which is alive

today and tomorrow is thrown into the furnace, will He not much more clothe you? You of little faith!

"Do not worry then, saying, 'What will we eat?' or 'What will we drink?' or 'What will we wear for clothing?' For the Gentiles eagerly seek all these things; for your heavenly Father knows that you need all these things.

"But seek first His kingdom and His righteousness, and all these things will be added to you. So do not worry about tomorrow; for tomorrow will care for itself. Each day has enough trouble of its own" (Matthew 6:25–34).

If you are a Christian, there is nothing that should prevent you from accepting Jesus' words as the absolute truth for keeping you free of anxiety and fear.

However, if you have never accepted Jesus Christ as Savior and Lord of your life, I want you to understand that there is no other way to God and eternal peace and joy except through Jesus.

So, whether you are reading this book because you are a cancer patient or because you simply want to know how you can help someone with cancer, I want you to know that the only way to achieve genuine relief from fear and anxiety is through God's only begotten Son.

If you wonder how I came to that conclusion, it was through the Word of God. *"Jesus said to him, 'I am the way, and the truth, and the life; no one comes to the Father but through Me'"* (John 14:6).

Right now might be the very best time for you to consider your eternal destiny. It could change more than your attitude.

God does not give us everything we want, but He does fulfill all His promises . . . leading us along the best and straightest paths to Himself.[2]

NOTES

1. *Worry Free Living,* Minirth/Meier.
2. Dietrich Bonhoeffer, German theologian (1906-1945).

chapter two
Faith Versus Fear

Fear is a normal human reaction, and typically what we fear the most is what we don't understand or know. It's been my observation that often we fear something in the future rather than in the present. Often, we fear the things that have yet to come upon us more than we fear the things we are presently going through. This is because, in the majority of cases, once the "things" arrive we are determined to handle them.

Reasons We Fear

A 19th century British Baptist minister, C.H. Spurgeon, said, "'Fear not, for I am with thee,' is God's sure word of promise to his chosen ones in the furnace of afflictions."

The question we have to ask is, "Why am I afraid?"

Since you're reading this book, one obvious reason for your fear is that either you have a disease like cancer or someone you care about does.

- *Fear of death.* Cancer not only has a bad reputation but also has a very bad track record, because many of the people who are diagnosed with cancer don't survive it. But you know what? The people who have perfect health don't survive that either. I want to keep reminding you, just as I continually remind myself, that nobody lives forever. We're all going to die from something.

- *Fear of the unknown.* If you or a loved one has been through surgery or some of the uncomfortable procedures related to cancer, you may also fear the many unknowns. Or you may simply fear the probable discomfort and pain. I can confirm that it does hurt to have parts cut from your body, but there are ways to deal with pain.

- *Fear of the lack of control.* Those who have cancer can attest to the fact that we are not in control of our lives when we have this disease. When I consider the accumulated hours I've spent in doctors' offices, wait-

ing for them to be able to see me, that is definitely experiencing a lack of control. For someone with a personality like mine, that is very difficult.

- *Fear of the financial cost.* You may have very good insurance, but the deductibles on the insurance can be
very costly. Then, there is the issue of a job loss that
can quickly spin a family into a financial hole that
could be difficult to overcome.

As Franklin D. Roosevelt once noted about the Great
Depression, "The only thing we have to fear is fear itself." I
believe that's true, because fear is simply the opposite of faith.
Faith is the belief in something greater than we are. *"Greater is
He who is in you than he who is in the world"* (1 John 4:4).

The Opposite of Fear

As a Christian, I believe in Jesus Christ as my Lord
and Savior. I have faith in God and believe that He is able to
do whatever He says. The Bible tells me that without faith it
is impossible to please God. Faith is clearly defined in the
New Testament as *"the assurance of things hoped for, the conviction of things not seen"* (Hebrews 11:1).

Understanding that what we hope and pray for and
being certain of what we do not see is very important, be-

cause that is *believing faith*. There's an entire world that exists around us that we do not see; it's known as the spirit world. We know it's there by faith, that is until we pass from this life into the next life. Then we'll know it's there by experience.

In God's Word, the spirit world is far more real than the world in which we live. It's been around longer, it's much more stable, and it will continue to be around much longer than this world.

Faith literally is the ability to believe, or accept, without doubting. Fear is opposite of faith: it brings on worry, frustration, and anxiety. Jesus tells us,

> *"Do not worry then, saying, 'What will we eat?' or 'What will we drink?' or 'What will we wear for clothing?' For the Gentiles eagerly seek all these things; for your heavenly Father knows that you need all these things. But seek first His kingdom and His righteousness, and all these things will be added to you. So do not worry about tomorrow; for tomorrow will care for itself. Each day has enough trouble of its own"* (Matthew 6:31–34).

For those of us who have experienced cancer, we would certainly all say "Amen!" to Jesus' words. Each day certainly does have enough trouble.

Afraid to Die

It has been my observation that as human beings we all have, to one degree or another, a fear of dying. I think it's built into us. We attach ourselves to people, houses, and autos. And, we attach ourselves to this life.

Our families fear that we will die, and that places a great burden on a cancer patient. One of the ways to overcome this fear of dying is to face death straight on. Let me give you an example.

For a long time I had a fear of flying. However, I did not realize that until I joined the Air Force and was flown from Florida to San Antonio, Texas. It was the first time I had flown, and I found that I didn't like being in the back of the plane while some pilot was totally in control of my life. It probably would have been okay with me if somehow I could have been up front and in control; then I might have loved flying. But my personality didn't lend itself to pacifism.

One of the ways I learned to overcome my fear of flying was to face it over and over and over again. Since then, I don't know how many miles I've flown, but I'd say it has been in excess of a million miles. Now I enjoy flying. I don't like flying in bad weather, being fogged in, or having mechanical problems, but I no longer fear flying.

When an aircraft breaks the sound barrier, it soars

with freedom. A Christian must break the death barrier while living, so that he or she can live without the haunting uncertainty and fear of dying.[1]

I accept my mortality as a fact of life. Perhaps as a younger person I chose to ignore it, but once you get past the halfway point you become more realistic. Furthermore, once you have cancer, you recognize that there's probably much less time left than what you have already spent.

The fear of dying is normal, but it must be faced, and the fear must be conquered. The way fear is conquered is to face it through faith in Jesus Christ. His promise to us is that *"I will never desert you, nor will I ever forsake you"* (Hebrews 13:5).

Your family must face fear with you. Fear is contagious, and if just one person around you is continually bemoaning your circumstance and is living in fear, it will spread throughout your family. Remember, "Death is a transition in eternal life, not a tragedy of termination."[2]

You must nip that sort of thing in the bud—through your faith—because faith is also contagious. When those around you observe you demonstrating your faith in Jesus Christ and see that you're willing to stand up to whatever it is God has for you to face, including this cancer, they're going to catch this attitude as well.

How to Trust God

Even if you can avoid dying from cancer, you'll certainly face something else that will eventually kill you, because all of us are going to die. As good as modern medicine is, it is not the ultimate answer. It will let you down. Trusting God is the answer. He will never let you down.

I'm not the kind of person who will take you through *three easy steps to trusting God,* because learning to trust God is not a 1,2,3-step process. Trusting God is really a gift of God.

"Raw dependence on the Lord to take care of us is a moment-by-moment risk. But He's worthy of the trust."[3]

Get to Know God

You get to know *about* God through His Word, but you get to *know* God by spending time alone with Him. The more I know about God the more I trust God, and the more I trust God the more I believe in and put my faith in Him totally. After all, there really isn't any other place to put your faith and trust anyway. Scripture tells us that *"faith comes from hearing, and hearing by the word of Christ"* (see Romans 10:8–17).

Let me repeat a fact that is absolutely true: We will all die eventually—every single one of us. I don't know what might help you to handle the reality of death, but for me it is faith. If you're young, it may be very difficult to face death, especially if you have a family with young children, because you probably fear leaving your family more than you fear death itself.

Satan is a great liar and deceiver, and he will tell you every lie possible, such as, "There is no God," "God doesn't care anything about you," "There is no eternity, and when you die there's nothing more." Those are all lies from the great liar.

As a Christian, once I realized and accepted my mortality and stopped fearing death, Satan stopped bothering me with the fear of death.

The truth is, if you believe in heaven, then death should not be a thing to fear. God wants us to live life to the fullest, but fear will cripple us. The issue isn't whether you have cancer or perfect health, because if there are circumstances that cause you to live in fear you can't possibly enjoy your life on this earth—no matter how healthy you are or how short or long your life may be. So, if you know that your final destination is heaven, then learn to live your life here to the fullest. F.B. Meyer says that "God incarnate is the end of fear."

When I was about 45 years old, we decided to move the ministry of Christian Financial Concepts out of Atlanta to a property near Dahlonega, Georgia. We planned to have a center where we would hold seminars and train volunteer budget and financial counselors.

We relocated the ministry and began to repair the run-down property. As the work progressed, we discovered one problem after another. I had a very busy schedule and would travel to teach seminars, then return to Georgia to find more problems than when I left. In the midst of this stressful time, through the wisdom of the Lord, the ministry was selected for an IRS audit. It was something called a technical compliance audit (very bad).

The IRS sent a man who had never audited a non-profit organization. He did not like Christians and clearly didn't trust anything Christian that bore the name "financial." He was committed to making my life about as miserable as one person can make another person's.

After about eight months of suffering though this time of auditing, traveling, coming back to find new problems with the property, and facing the IRS auditor who was constantly harassing us, I found myself experiencing burnout. I was going down in an emotional tailspin, unable to think clearly. Sometimes I had difficulty functioning at all.

I was still able to teach, because I'd done it so much that I could do it almost automatically; but I was miserable and fearful—about everything. I realized that the fear was based on dread of the IRS finding something I had missed and then shutting down the ministry.

I knew that was wrong so I confessed the fear to God, but I still couldn't get out of the depression. I had allowed myself to get so far downhill emotionally that I could no longer control my emotions.

Just before Christmas I went to teach a conference in New York. I was in such bad shape that the people there recognized it, and they ministered to me much more than I was able to minister to them.

I felt like I was at the very bottom. I went home and took some time off to regroup, but I still couldn't seem get out from under the pressure. It wasn't until my second son, Dan, had an automobile accident that I began to get out from under the stress and depression I was suffering.

Our son was in a coma. Judy and I sat in the hospital day after day, night after night. His life was hanging precariously in the balance. Several times nurses or doctors came to warn us that Dan might die at any moment.

Slowly, I began to realize that the problems that had gotten me down weren't that great. I discovered that our son Dan was much more important than any IRS audit, the ministry being shut down, or whether I ever taught again.

While I was totally focused on my son, I began to turn outward, and I started to share the Lord with other parents whose children were lying there in the hospital. Many wouldn't listen because they didn't want to hear about Christianity—until they learned that our son had been in a coma for several months. Then they began to talk, and I discovered that my stress and depression evaporated. I stopped living in fear and, once again, began living by faith.

Later, that lesson became a tremendous benefit when I was diagnosed with cancer.

Love Conquers Fear—Every Time

I readily admit that discovering I had cancer was a shock. No one in my family had had cancer, and I found myself wondering if this was "it." After I learned how severe my cancer was, I said, "Okay, I might die." The exciting thing to me was that I had no fear, because I was living by faith in the One who had first loved me.

Jesus Christ is God's perfect example of perfect love. Those who come to know Him as Lord of their lives understand this. The Scriptures bear testimony of the power of love over fear. *"There is no fear in love; but perfect love casts out fear, because fear involves punishment, and the one who fears is not perfected in love. We love, because He first loved us"* (1 John 4:18–19).

Corrie Ten Boom said, "There is no darkness that Satan can create that can shut the love of God out." If you find yourself worrying about your health, whether it's cancer or something else, and you are living in fear, Satan's got you. You need to shake that attitude—now.

Let me tell you about the effect of fear. Jesus was walking on the water one night when His disciples were in a boat.

> *"When the disciples saw Him walking on the sea, they were terrified, and said, 'It is a ghost!' And they cried out in fear. But immediately Jesus spoke to them, saying, 'Take courage, it is I; do not be afraid.' Peter said to Him, 'Lord, if it is You, command me to come to You on the water.' And He said, 'Come!' And Peter got out of the boat, and walked on the water and came toward Jesus. But seeing the wind, he became frightened, and beginning to sink, he cried out, 'Lord, save me!' Immediately Jesus stretched out His hand and took hold of him, and said to him, 'You of little faith, why did you doubt?'"* (Matthew 14:26–31).

I think that could have been any one of us. It doesn't have to be walking on the water; it may be walking through cancer or walking down the hospital corridor to a cancer patient's room. The simple truth is, when you're walking through cancer or any other storm of life, Jesus will hold His hand out and say, "*Come.*"

Then, as we begin to walk through the process, we

become involved with doctors, hospitals, surgery, radiation, chemotherapy, and all the other scary things that happen; and we might begin to doubt. That's when we begin to sink. Nevertheless, remember that the way to get out of that sinking situation is to reach back up and take Jesus' hand. He'll be there and He will ask, *"Why did you doubt?"* You see, He is always there for those who believe. Don't doubt. Have faith, and trust in God.

The Lord doesn't ridicule us for our fears. He walks through them with us. As Corrie Ten Boom said, "Do not be afraid to trust an unknown future to a known God."

Fear and Your Immune System

It may be a surprise to learn that your attitude can directly affect your immune system.

When you laugh and have fun, you release endorphins and hormones that make your body feel better and help you relax. Laughing also stimulates your immune system. So, if you'll refuse to mope around and will have some fun, enjoy yourself, and laugh a bit, you'll feel better physically. Henry Ward Beecher wrote that "Mirth is God's medicine. Everybody ought to bathe in it. Grim care, moroseness, anxiety—all this rust of life—ought to be scoured off by the oil of mirth."

The opposite is true as well. If you live in fear and anxiety and allow negatives to rule, it will suppress your immune system and you'll become even more vulnerable to cancer and to other secondary diseases as well. According to Edmund Burke, "No passion so effectually robs the mind of all its powers of acting and reasoning as fear."

Negative thoughts and emotions tend to compound themselves. Fear and anxiety can come from many sources, including health, business, family, or other pressures. The cause of the fear and anxiety doesn't matter, because the result is the same: your immune system becomes suppressed, and you become an easy target for disease.

So the best thing you can do for yourself is live by faith—not fear. Fear numbs your mind and dulls your creativeness. I consider myself a creative person, but I can remember that when I was in that burnout period my creativity was almost nonexistent. In the midst of a cancer battle, one of the things you need is a lot of creativity.

Remember that *you* are responsible for your health; the doctors are not. They can provide consultation, knowledge, advice, and procedures, but you must ultimately make your own decisions, and to do that you must keep your creativity level high.

Fear also disrupts your life and numbs your ability to have pleasure. I don't mind having cancer as much as I mind the way cancer interrupts my life. In my case, the surgeries I went through have been an infringement in my life, because the pain from those surgeries is still with me, and it has limited my ability to do some things. However, I've learned to work around them.

"Staying calm in the face of [fear] danger is your best defense. Worrying about what might happen causes unnecessary stress. So relax, and remember you're in God's hands."[4]

Bear in mind that fear can actually kill you. I've talked to people with cancer whom I believe would have survived if they had simply changed their attitudes, developed positive outlooks, and put their trust in the Lord. I can think of at least 10 people who might be alive today if they had not had such negative attitudes. They were so angry and fearful that they simply emotionally curled up in a dark corner of their minds and physically died.

Obviously, no one in his or her right mind would look forward to suffering, but think of what God's Word promises: *"Consider it all joy, my brethren, when you encounter various trials, knowing that the testing of your faith produces endurance. And let endurance have its perfect result, so that you may be perfect and complete, lacking in nothing"* (James 1:2–4).

When you face trials, it is so important to remember that if you'll face them in a godly way and trust the Lord you'll find that, according to God's Word, you'll develop endurance: the ability to stand resolutely—without failing.

"In times of affliction we commonly meet with the

sweetest experiences of the love of God."[5] Although I don't believe God caused my trial with cancer, I do believe He has allowed me to have cancer for the purpose of maturing me. As a result of that, if I am willing I will have the opportunity to direct many other people to the Lord, because I am becoming a more mature Christian as a result of the cancer experience.

As a result of sharing God's truth with people with cancer or whose loved ones had cancer, in the last eight years I have introduced more people to the Lord, one on one, than in the previous 26-year period as a believer. Perhaps that's the purpose of these trials. However, if you allow fear to overcome your faith, your witness will suffer, because few people listen to the witness of a fearful Christian.

The Effects of Faith

Faith boosts your immune system. It allows you to enjoy the life you have. None of us are guaranteed more time than the day we have today. Christians are going to spend eternity with God. It grieves me to see believers who have lost sight of that fact. During the stress of traumatic circumstances of any kind, it's important to remember that *this* life is the worst situation we should expect. If you are a believer, the worst thing that can happen to you is that you die and go to heaven; and that is something to look forward to!

Through faith, God wants you enjoy life. Realistically, my cancer should have killed me years ago. Nevertheless, I find myself enjoying life more than ever, and the little things just don't bother me, because I don't sweat the small stuff. I don't have a left shoulder blade, but I'm still able to play golf. Nobody understands that, especially the people that I'm able to beat when playing golf, and I have humiliated a few pretty good golfers by beating them with one arm.

God allows you to enjoy life. Life isn't over just because you have cancer. Faith provides the opportunity to witness to other people and faith strengthens your spiritual power as well. As a result of witnessing to so many people, I've had to reconfirm my own belief system. I've discovered that I have to decide if I *really do believe* some of the things I write and say, or do I just *say I believe.*

If you live in fear, anger, and anxiety because you have cancer, you won't do much witnessing to others about the grace of God, because you aren't experiencing God's grace yourself.

A good friend of mine had kidney cancer before I did. In the early stages of his cancer he ran to and fro looking at everything available: doctors, traditional treatments, and alternative treatments. After about three years he realized that he was going to die of cancer. Instead of waiting to die, he went back to teaching Bible studies as God had called him to do. He decided by faith to live his life to the fullest. That's what God wants us to do.

Don't let the fear of the time it will take to accomplish something stand in the way of your doing it. The time will pass anyway; we might just as well put that passing time to the best possible use.[6]

I recall a Chinese pastor I met many years ago. He had been confined in solitary imprisonment for over 30 years—simply because he was a Christian and had shared his faith openly. One of the greatest testimonies of his life was that he had led dozens of guards and others to the Lord, and he didn't do it from a radio broadcasting studio or a fancy pulpit. He led people to faith in Jesus Christ through a locked cell door, as he shared the message of God's truth for 30 years. That's what I call a life well lived, not a life lived in fear.

That reminds me of another example. Perhaps you'll remember Martin Burnham, the New Tribes missionary pilot who, along with his wife, Gracia, was held hostage in the Philippines by the Abu Sayyaf Group. He was ultimately killed in a military action that also injured his wife. Gracia said that each night when the guard came to chain Martin to a tree, Martin would say "Thank you" and wish his guards a good evening. He witnessed to them at every opportunity. He did not live in fear.

I encourage you to take God's offer to heart: to believe in the Lord Jesus Christ and be saved. Begin today to live by faith and you won't have to live in fear.

God Knows

Remember that doctors don't know everything, so don't listen to negative talk. Don't ask anyone, including your doctors, "How long do you think I'll live?" The person you're asking doesn't know the answer. Only God knows that.

After being diagnosed with cancer, I met a man with pancreatic cancer who has become a good friend. Pancreatic cancer is presumed to always be fatal, usually very rapidly. Every time my friend goes to see a doctor he's told that he has only six months to live. They've been telling him that for 11 years. He travels back and forth to Russia several times a year to share his faith. If he had believed what the doctors said about his life expectancy, he might never have gone to share his faith in Russia.

It's amazing to me that I have had five or six friends who (as far as they knew) were totally healthy before I was diagnosed with cancer, but they have since died. So, don't let anyone tell you that you'll die at a certain time. Only God knows that. He decides who lives and who dies, how long we live, and when we die.

If you notice that you're getting down spiritually, emotionally, or mentally, find a friend who walks the talk in his or her faith. Kay Arthur says, "Faith recognizes that God is in control, not man. Faith does it God's way, in God's timing—according to His good pleasure."

Get involved with helping other people if you are physically able to do so. You'll find that your troubles won't seem nearly so bad. Spend some time outside yourself. Make it a point to lift up someone else.

I talk to people with cancer all the time. Sometimes their problems get me down, especially when I talk to someone with my type of cancer whom I know is dying. I suppose that's because I begin to think *that could happen to me.* Know what? That's exactly right. Except for the grace of God, there go I.

But I'm happy to add that more than a few of these cancer patients have fooled me. They didn't die as I supposed and are today cancer free. It just affirms what I keep saying: Only God knows the day and the time.

What About Drugs?

I don't need mood levelers, but if I needed them I wouldn't hesitate to take something to help me through a difficult time. If that's what you need, find a doctor who knows how to do the most with the least.

It seems to me there's a lot of hypocrisy among Christians when it comes to using drugs to alter an emotional or mental condition. I've not met a Christian with diabetes who didn't take insulin if that was required or a Christian with a serious infection who wouldn't take an antibiotic. Why then, if our bodies need these helpful drugs from time to time, do we think our minds might not also need appropriate help from a drug? If you need drugs because of cancer, it is not a sin to take what you need for help. I see nothing that prohibits that in Scripture.

Prayer Works

Pray often; for prayer is a shield to the soul, a sacrifice to God, and a scourge for Satan.[7] I encourage you also to ask friends and family to pray for you regularly. Nothing boosts my spirits more than having someone tell me that he or she is praying for me every day. There are people who will not only say that but will actually do it.

I rather suspect that a hundred years from now your health problems and mine will seem petty. Keep that in mind, trust God, stay positive, and live by faith. Don't live in fear.

NOTES

1. Lloyd Ogilvie, chaplain of the U.S. Senate.
2. Ibid.
3. Ibid.

4. From *God's Little Lessons on Life,* Honor Book, p. 79.
5. John Bunyan, English preacher and author.
6. Earl Nightingale, motivational speaker.
7. John Bunyan, English preacher and author.

chapter three
Finding the Right Treatment

If there is one certainty, it's that the practice of medicine is exactly that: *practicing*. Medical research is constantly changing and being upgraded, new technologies are coming out all the time, and new therapies are continually being offered. And there are many alternatives when it comes to dealing with a disease as difficult as cancer—or more correctly, diseases. Cancer is not one disease; it is many.

For many people there are simply too many alternatives available. I regularly get calls from people who have been diagnosed with cancer, have gone through the traditional therapies that were available to them, and now find that they have a recurrence of their cancer. Thus, they're looking around to see what other treatments are available.

Often, they are overwhelmed with the choices

available to them, because everybody gives them advice. Many advocate alternative therapies, others want them to stick with traditional therapies, and some recommend that they travel to Europe for therapy—like I did. The choices are so many and so varied, people are totally bewildered, unless they are either dedicated researchers or have others who will do the research for them.

How It All Started

If you find yourself being overwhelmed with the apparent choices available, perhaps I can help. Let me walk you back through my experience.

Many of those who read this book may have read my first book, *Hope When It Hurts* (first published as *Damaged But Not Broken,* Moody). It dealt with the personal journey that Judy and I have had as a result of my cancer. Some of what I am going to tell you will be repetitious, so forgive me. For others who are reading this as a first book about cancer, it might help for me to summarize my diagnosis and treatment.

As you read, keep in mind that I had never even thought about the possibility of having cancer prior to hearing my diagnosis. No one had ever had cancer on either side of my family. My father died of a heart attack, and most of his brothers died of heart attacks as well. So, I was very conscious of heart disease and cholesterol, but I had absolutely no concern for cancer. I thought many times, *Well we Burketts may die of heart attacks, but at least we have some kind of an immunity to cancer.* Ha! Not so.

In May of 1993, I decided to learn to play golf, because most of my brothers played. At the time I was about 54, probably not a good age to take up a new sport. One of the things I found as I began to practice was that my left shoulder began to hurt—not all that unusual at my age. The pain initially was not very severe, but as time went along the pain became more frequent and intense.

In December 1994, the nagging pain noticeably worsened while we were at our cabin in North Carolina. I was chopping wood for the fireplace and had a very severe pain in my left shoulder—so severe that I couldn't move my left arm for a period of time. I knew at that point that I needed to find out what my problem was.

About a month later I was out playing golf with my stepfather. I swung at the ball and had exactly the same thing happen again: I felt a pop in my left shoulder and the pain prevented me from lifting my arm.

I began the normal routine and saw an orthopedist in the town where I live—Gainesville, Georgia. Then, to get other opinions, I visited two other orthopedists. One diagnosed the problem as a potential rotator cuff tear, and the other said the problem was bursitis.

Ultimately I went to still another orthopedist, who diagnosed my problem as a difficulty with my collarbone. Actually, I had broken my collarbone playing high school football and it had healed slightly misaligned. This orthopedist believed the pain was caused by the misalignment of the collarbone, since that interfered with the action of the shoulder blade.

That made more sense to me than the other diagnoses did, so I decided that was the one I would accept. Although he suggested surgery to correct the problem, I elected not to do so immediately, even though at that time I believed that ultimately I would have to schedule it.

I had a friend who was a well-known heart bypass surgeon at Emory University in Atlanta. I called him and asked whom he would see at Emory if he had my problem, and he referred me to a sports orthopedist. When I went to the Emory sports clinic, it was the first time a doctor recommended having an MRI—so he could look inside the shoulder to see exactly what was going on.

In February 1995, while we were at our cabin in North Carolina, I received a call from Emory University Hospital and the caller said, "The doctors have examined the MRI and believe you need to come back right away to be checked."

I asked her what they thought the problem was. She was very hesitant but then said, "It appears to be a small mass under your left scapula [shoulder blade]."

Isn't it interesting the terms that physicians use? Instead of saying "tumor" or "cancer" they say *"small mass,"* which sounds ominous and could be anything.

Well, we packed up and hurried back to Atlanta. After talking with the doctor, he was fairly certain that what I had was a tumor. But, because he could not be sure if it was malignant, he suggested that I have a CT scan (computerized thermograph scan)—to look through the rest of my body to see if there was anything out of place.

I did that, and the diagnosis from the CT scan revealed that I had kidney cancer, on the upper pole of my right kidney, and the cancer had metastasized (spread) to my left shoulder blade. Further tests revealed that there was only a single metastasis visible. The doctor's recommendation was simple: take out the right kidney and then remove the left shoulder blade.

When something like this happens, a person is usually not thinking very clearly and relies totally on the physician's recommendation. If I had realized at the time that I didn't have to rush, I probably would have taken a lot more time to explore the options that might have been available— other than removing my shoulder blade. Of course, I knew that my shoulder blade was a very necessary part of my body, but I didn't realize until later just how much its removal would affect everything I do.

In March of 1995, I went into Emory University Hospital and had a radical right nephrectomy. My right kidney was removed, along with all the associated paraphernalia: the adrenal gland, the ductwork going to the bladder, and everything attached to my kidney. They also removed a margin around the area as well, because they knew that it had metastasized and wanted to see if the lymph nodes in those areas were involved.

In my case, the diagnosis showed that the cancer was contained in the kidney and had not metastasized to the lymph glands, as far as they could tell. Even so, we knew it was metastatic, because of the tumor in my left shoulder blade.

Two weeks after the nephrectomy, I was admitted to another hospital associated with Emory, and there an orthopedic surgeon removed my left scapula. I'm one of only a few people in America who have had a radical scapulectomy. There are probably not a dozen in our country who have undergone this surgery, and now I understand why.

The pathology report on the tumor from my scapula showed that it was metastatic renal cell carcinoma.

My Next Step

About two weeks after the shoulder surgery I went back to talk to my primary physician, who was the head of urology at Emory. He is a really fine doctor and a super guy. I asked him what my alternatives were. By this time I had been looking around and doing a little research and realized that for metastatic renal cell carcinoma there were very few alternatives—except to die. More than 95 percent of those who are diagnosed with metastatic renal cell carcinoma die within two years, because the disease is relentless.

Fortunately, my doctor was very honest with me. He said, "We do have some experimental treatments that primarily involve immune boosting therapies, such as interferon and interleukin and others, but we've not found them to be particularly effective. If I were you, I'd look elsewhere. You've got some time to look around, because you only had the single metastasis, and we have removed the kidney and shoulder blade."

I asked him what I should look for. "Well," he replied, "relatively speaking, there are very few cases of kidney cancer, only about 30 to 50 thousand cases a year and that includes all types of kidney cancer, whether isolated or metastatic. It will be difficult to find much data on kidney cancer therapy, and it may be pretty unfruitful."

However, he also recommended that I look for treatments for another type of cancer that generally responds similarly to kidney cancer. That turned out be melanoma.

Melanoma is generally associated with skin cancers, a

result of lengthy exposure to the sun. Most melanomas are successfully removed, but if they spread or if the surgeon doesn't remove them completely many times melanomas will come back as lung cancer or tumors in other parts of the body.

My doctor explained that the treatment for melanoma is very similar to the treatment for kidney cancer, because they both respond primarily to immune therapy. Both are resistant to chemotherapy and somewhat resistant to radiation, except in very high doses.

I took that to heart. Since there are millions of cases of melanoma annually here in the United States and around the world, I decided that's where I would focus my primary search. My daughter Kimberly is very similar in personality to me. She enjoys doing research and began doing most of the research for me, because at that time I was not feeling at all well. We found there was a lot of information available on the Internet.

Interestingly enough, the treatment that I chose was one that had been used with both melanoma and kidney cancer. The choices are seldom so clear cut.

By sheer happenstance (looking back, I see it was God's sovereign plan for me), a physician friend in Gainesville told me of a friend named Jim Baker who had melanoma and had gone to Europe for immune therapy.

I contacted Jim, and Judy and I went to the Baker's

home. They graciously received us and we sat and chatted for several hours. I found Jim to be an intelligent man and very open. He had developed skin cancer and had it removed. Then, seven years later he was playing tennis when he collapsed. The doctors diagnosed him with lung cancer. Unfortunately they misdiagnosed the type of lung cancer he had and he underwent surgery for adino carcinoma, which did more harm than good. After a short recovery he made contact with someone who had gone to Prague in the Czech Republic, and he soon followed through with the immune therapy.

I wasted no time in contacting the Prague clinic by telephone and was able to talk with the only English speaking person in the laboratory. I discovered that the therapy had been in existence for more than 20 years, and it had actually started in Greece. The doctor who developed it died and a physician from Prague, who had been working with him, brought the therapy back to Prague to further develop it.

Off to Prague

That was about the time that communism fell in Europe. Prague was a great place to locate the clinic, because they had so many highly specialized scientists, biophysicists, and molecular biologists who were unemployed.

I discovered that several hundred patients had taken the therapy—many from the United States. I made contact with about a dozen of them who had been treated for melanoma, but I found none who had been treated for renal cell carcinoma.

Of the 12 people I called, two had died. Nevertheless, family members said they had lived longer than anyone thought they would, and they had a better quality of life as a result of having gone through the treatment.

Of the 10 who were still alive, all had been diagnosed in this country as terminal and given a very short time to live, but all 10 were still alive.

It made sense to me. There were other therapies available, and I'm sure some might have been helpful. But none had the quality of personnel that I found in Prague. After Judy and I prayed about it, we decided to go to Prague so I could do the immune therapy.

Others I spoke to had gone to places like Mexico and the Bahamas for different immune therapies. Over the years I have been asked why I didn't go to one of those closer locations where they had similar immune therapies, since they certainly would have been less expensive. The reason I didn't was that I felt that quality control was not as good in these countries as it was in Prague.

Additionally, I did not have the time to sort through the treatments that were not good, and I decided to go to Europe, where I felt the standards of quality and personnel were much higher. They had been around a long time, and I believed the margin for error would be lower there.

So, we went to Prague and spent about one month doing the immune therapy. While there, we also began to help the clinic get the therapy treatment approved in the United States. We were able to help them make the appropriate medical contacts, and the therapy now has been approved through the FDA investigative review board process. Now any licensed physician in America can sign up to do the therapy.

Nevertheless, the vast majority of physicians do not use it; they don't understand how it works or why it works. By U.S. standards, there's not sufficient clinical data available.

From 1995 to 1997 I settled into a routine of changing my diet. One of the first changes I made was to begin drinking filtered and ozonated water. I don't know if that change was necessary, but it was one of those things that I could change. I became a vegetarian, although not an absolute vegetarian. I eat some white meat, fish, and turkey. This allows me to maintain an adequate protein level, while avoiding most products that have been hormonally enhanced. I will discuss my reasons for dieting this way in the chapter dealing with nutrition.

Designing a Plan

At my doctor's suggestion, I also settled into a routine of having a CT scan every six months, screening the chest, thorax, and abdomen. This procedure helps to determine if other tumors have developed. With the normal prognosis of renal cell carcinoma, additional metastatic tumors are expected.

About every 18 months I also have a bone scan, because renal cell carcinoma often shows up in the bones. Early detection is essential, because cancer rarely sends signals until significant destruction has taken place.

In seeking the right treatment, I have researched other diagnostic tools that will help determine if I have the cancer. There are tools, like the proton emission scan (PET scan), and several other blood tests that have been developed that can detect evidence of cancer before the tumors can be seen on traditional scans.

During my second set of CT scans in November 1997, two suspicious areas showed up: one in the *hilar* region between the lungs and the other in the inferior *vena cava* region, next to the main artery just below my breastbone.

When tumors are developing and standard diagnostic tools like CT scans are used, the scans often can't detect the tumor until it is about 1.5 mm in size. That means a smaller tumor could be developing undetected.

In my case, that proved to be true. Initially the scan showed two slightly enlarged lymph nodes. Several radiologists disagreed about whether it was simply an infection being fought by the lymph nodes or if it meant cancer.

In early 1998, when subsequent CT scans were examined, the consensus opinion was that two lymph nodes were infected with renal cell carcinoma—not good news.

Again, those who have cancer will sometimes get bad reports. That's when faith really matters, and it is necessary to turn both the positives *and* the negatives over to the Lord. That's exactly what I did. I turned the bad news over to God.

Even though I wasn't going to worry about it, I wanted to be as wise as I could, so I decided to look for whatever treatments were available to me. I knew I would resort to surgery *only* if there were no other alternatives available. Having gone through two really debilitating surgeries, I didn't want to repeat surgery unless I absolutely had to.

In this case, when the nodes showed up I didn't change my established protocol; I just started adding things to it. I continued the scans, the immune therapy, and good nutrition, and I exercised as well as I could. Whenever I would hear or read about treatments or technologies that sounded reasonable, I would check on them and pursue them if they were within reason.

Whenever I would come across something new, I

would use my own criteria to determine if I would pursue it further. I tell about that criteria in more detail in Chapter 5.

From 1998 through 2000 I did a variety of things, one of which was an ex-vivos T cell stimulation. T cells are the primary disease fighters of the body—cells that migrate from the bone marrow and mature in the *thymus,* which accounts for their designation as "T" cells.

I went to a hospital in Memphis, Tennessee, where a cancer therapy group from Boston was doing clinical studies. I'd fly to Memphis once a week and they would do an *apheresis* (the separation of blood into its individual components), where they would extract T cells from me. Those T cells were then externally stimulated in *interleukin* (a protein made naturally by the body) to help boost the immune system.

Periodically I would return to Memphis, and the supercharged T cells would be reinserted into my blood.

The theory behind all this sounded very good to me. The scientists would extract, let's say, a billion T cells from me (these are relative numbers). They would then put them in the external solution of *interleukin* and grow them until there were 100 billion T cells (again the numbers are relative and are actually much larger).

These disease-killing cells had been produced externally and, when returned to my body (theoretically), they would seek and kill the cancer cells. These were not "targeted"

T cells—that is, they were just general T cells that would go everywhere in my body fighting disease and, of course, some T cells would specialize and fight the cancer.

The theory certainly seemed sound. Unfortunately, I was about halfway through that therapy when a larger pharmaceutical company bought the pharmaceutical company that was conducting the study and shut it down. I have no idea of the reasoning behind this, although my theory is that the therapy was going to compete with the drugs already being offered by the larger pharmaceutical company. Such is life in America.

Next I tried a therapy in Tennessee that had been developed at the nuclear research facility in Oak Ridge. It was a magnetic therapy, and the idea was that high levels of magnetism would reverse the polarity of diseased cells, such as cancerous cells, and render them ineffective.

Unfortunately, I was about one-fourth of the way through that therapy when the Food and Drug Administration (FDA) raided the facility, confiscated all the equipment and records, and this therapy also was shut down.

About mid-1999 I met a doctor in South Georgia who had been attracted to Georgia because of the change in the law that allows a patient to take any therapy for cancer as long as it is under the control of a licensed physician. This doctor was working with a molecular biologist who had a cancer treatment he had been working on for the better part of 25 years. He was a multiple Ph.D. scientist who had worked with the National Cancer Institute for many years and had moved to Georgia to apply his theory.

He would extract T cells that were to be targeted specifically to my cancer. They would be "trained" externally by exposing them to a solution that contained cancer cells from my tumor and then would attack the cancer when reinserted into my blood stream.

The idea seemed sound, and he had obtained effective results on other types of cancer. He had a researcher from Emory University documenting his tests. Thus, he had good research and good data, so I started that therapy around the middle of 1999. I thought it had great promise and, in fact, I responded well to the therapy.

The supporting lab conducted immune system tests before extraction and after re-infusion of the T cells, and my system responded well to the therapy. The number of killer cells that were targeted toward my tumor was going up exponentially. Unfortunately, about halfway through this therapy the doctor died of a heart attack. As a result, the whole program was discontinued.

Apparently God did not want me to have one of these silver bullets to kill my cancer.

Don't Give Up

You will recall that I found most of these therapies on the Internet—information that is available to anyone who is willing to do the research. I had two things going for me: I like to do research and so I investigated therapies on the Internet a lot, and also my insurance company was cooperative enough that they at least paid for the traditional tests.

About this time I read about a radiologist in Mississippi, Dr. Patrick Sewell at the University of Mississippi Medical College (UMMC) in Jackson, who was killing tumors by using a method called cryogenic ablation. He inserted needles into the tumors and then used a freezing liquid to kill the tumors by freezing them. For tumors that were not as accessible or not easily killed by freezing, he would use radiofrequency therapy to literally fry them.

About 1998 I sent him a copy of my CT scans and asked if he thought he could remove my tumors with his therapy if it became necessary. His response was that he could, but my tumors would be difficult, especially since a new tumor had appeared on my remaining kidney. However, he asked me to stay in contact with him, which I did. Periodically I would send copies of my CT scans and ask for his evaluation.

After the doctor who had been doing the vaccine

therapy died, I realized that I had to do something. The tumor that had showed up on my kidney in 1998 began to grow. Fortunately, my doctors said that the tumors were growing very slowly, apparently because I was doing good immune therapy and my immune system was able to control them somewhat. This gave me some precious time.

By 2001 I felt that I had exhausted my alternatives. I had tried several alternative treatments that had been stopped for the reasons I have mentioned. I realized that I had to either have the tumors resected surgically or find another method to have them removed.

I Found Mine

I contacted Dr. Sewell at UMMC in July 2001, sent him the most recent CT scans, and asked if he thought it was now time to freeze my tumors. By that time he had been doing his procedures for about two-and-one-half years. His research assistant called me and said that Dr. Sewell was now ready to see me. By this time he had removed tumors from 56 kidneys.

The tumor that was going to be most difficult to remove was the one between the lungs. Before contacting Dr. Sewell, I had gone to several surgeons to ask their opinions. Almost without exception, they said I would have to be split open, as if doing open-heart surgery, then have the right lung removed before the tumor could be removed.

I said, "I don't think so. I think I would rather die than do that." As I said before, because of the life I have in Jesus Christ, my opinion is that death is a reward from God, not a punishment. It is a triumphant transition. Don't misunderstand me. I want to stay here as long as I can, but I'm not going to disable myself and thus be prevented from doing what God has called me to do—just so I can stay here. The choice is mine.

In November 2001 I went to Jackson, Mississippi, and Dr. Sewell froze the tumor on my kidney and the one in the *vena cava* area. I was under general anesthesia for about 12 hours and the only recovery needed was from the effect of the anesthesia. After one week I felt pretty good again.

The next month I returned to Jackson. This time Dr. Sewell used radiofrequency ablation and killed the tumor between my lungs in the *hilar* region. He went through the left lung with the needle; then, using an array of expanding needles, he "fried" it. The tumor dried up like a raisin.

I should explain that the procedures called cryoablation and radiofrequency ablation do not actually remove the tumors; instead they kill the tumors. Then after a period of time the tumors shrivel up and the body assimilates most of the tissue.

Nevertheless, there is usually some residual evidence of the tumor. It takes a very astute radiologist to read the CT scans and render an appropriate diagnosis to determine whether the tissue is alive or dead.

In God's Word we're told,

> *"Let endurance have its perfect result, so that you may be perfect and complete, lacking in nothing. But if any of you lacks wisdom, let him ask of God, who gives to all generously and without reproach, and it will be given to him. But he must ask in faith without any doubting, for the one who doubts is like the surf of the sea, driven and tossed by the wind. For that man ought not to expect that he will receive anything from the Lord, being a double-minded man, unstable in all his ways"* (James 1:4–8).

I absolutely believe that promise and believe that when I pray for wisdom God will give it to me. Wisdom is not knowledge; wisdom is the application of knowledge, and wisdom comes only from God. Charles Stanley says that having "real common sense means you know that God is the source of wisdom."

I pray that God will give me the wisdom to know what to do and when to do it and that He will not allow me to have fear in the process, because fear paralyzes. God has been so gracious to Judy and me and has provided us with

His wisdom regularly. I believe that finding Dr. Sewell was God's answer to my prayer for His wisdom.

"People are yearning to see how Christ can make stepping stones out of their struggles. What they need to hear and see is the difference Christ can make in a person's life," says Lloyd Ogilvie.

I want you to know that God is waiting to answer your prayers and provide you with the same peace, freedom from fear, and assurance of His leading and wisdom too. He has provided the way for you to do just that through His Son, the Lord Jesus Christ.

Many of the other things I have done and am still doing, such as the immune therapies, are not cures. They are treatments, and they do a good job of controlling the growth until I can find a way to destroy the tumors.

If I had had a tumor removed from my kidney, another from my stomach area, and yet another from between my lungs under traditional surgery, it would have been extremely costly, very painful, and would have shut me down for months, if not forever. Instead, Dr. Sewell did his procedure on Tuesday, I was released Wednesday, stayed in my motel room Thursday, and drove home Friday. The main reason I was out of commission at all was because of the anesthesia.

For the second procedure, to remove the tumor from

between my lungs, Dr. Sewell did the procedure on Tuesday, I was released from the hospital Wednesday, and drove home Thursday, with no recovery time. I didn't play golf Friday, but I did play the following Monday. What a marvelous procedure, as compared to cutting me wide open to remove tumors.

Obviously this procedure isn't available to everyone. There are limitations as with any procedure, and Dr. Sewell and his small staff are overworked. I pray that enough resources will be directed to his research so that this technology, and its availability, will be expanded.

I really believe I've lived long enough that technology has caught up to my problem. Perhaps that was God's plan, to keep me around to help Dr. Sewell spread the awareness of this great technological asset throughout the world.

Or, perhaps God had me go through all that I have gone through for the purpose of sharing with other people and helping to reduce some of the misery and pain associated with cancer. Hopefully, in the next few years we'll not only find treatment for these cancers but cures will be found as well. In the meantime, you need to stay alive.

While I was looking for the right treatment, I tried a variety of things that just didn't work for me. I've tried nutritional plans offered by Christians, a variety of supplements, and even the very complicated therapy from the doctor in

Helsinki, Finland. Most of them simply didn't fit my personal lifestyle.

I've tried not to get discouraged by those that don't seem suitable for me. You will have failures, and some things that worked for me may not work for you, but you must not become discouraged.

Someone once asked Thomas Edison, "How can you stay so intense in trying to find the right filament for an electric light bulb? You've failed 260 times so far." Edison looked at the person and with a smile said, "I have never failed. I have simply found 260 things that don't work." He later said, "I am not discouraged, because every wrong attempt discarded is another step forward."

That has to be your attitude, otherwise you'll become discouraged and give up. When you stay discouraged you get depressed; then your immune system shuts down, and that's not what you want.

And You Can Find Yours

So, where do you go and how do you find the right therapy for you? Start by asking all your family and friends to help. Let them know you're researching your cancer, because you need to know your cancer well if you're going to defeat it.

Get on the Internet and, using a good search engine,

start your hunt for information. (I use *Google,* but there are many others.) Type in the description of your cancer. If you have liver cancer, melanoma, or breast cancer, type that. You'll discover hundreds of articles—many written by qualified experts, some by patients, and others by quacks. It's up to you (perhaps with the help of a family member) to sort them out. Be sure to look for those with good credentials.

Ask your friends to send you copies of articles they read about cancer, even if they're not about your specific disease. If you keep them aware of your need for data, you'll be amazed how many of your family and friends will respond.

Do not despair. You can find someone who will help with this research. Perhaps your spouse, child, grandchild, family member, or a friend likes to do research. God has someone in your life just waiting for you to ask for his or her help.

The Internet is a great tool—use it!

Look for research done by licensed physicians or research hospitals—not for someone who graduated from some unknown university with a degree that was bought for $30 through the mail or over the Internet.

When I've seen names repeated and quoted frequently during research, I've found that these were typically researchers. Occasionally I have participated in a cancer patient chat room. I usually limited myself to kidney cancer;

but, because melanoma is so close, I'd sometimes go to a melanoma chat room and just ask questions.

Good therapies and good treatments are only part of this equation. You can have the best treatments and therapies available and still die. The other part of the equation is that you must have peace in your life, enjoy your life, and trust in the Lord.

Outside of Jesus Christ, all the rest is irrelevant. You can have the best therapies in the world, be cured of your cancer, and live another 25 years, but you still will die. And, ultimately, you will spend eternity either with God or separated from Him. I want to go to be with God and I have the assurance of that happening in my life, because of my faith in Jesus Christ.

As I have mentioned earlier, perhaps the reason God has allowed me to go through all of this pain and suffering is simply to be able to help you. But if all I do is help you find the appropriate treatment for your disease (as beneficial as that may be), I haven't really done what God has put me here to do.

An even more essential need you have—more than a cure for your cancer—is what God wants for you in Jesus Christ. It is only through receiving Him as your Lord and Savior that you can have eternal peace, and through God's grace you can have the freedom from fear that you seek in this lifetime. C.S. Lewis said, "The Son of God became man to enable men to become the sons of God."

Jesus said to His followers, *"These things I have spoken to you, so that in Me you may have peace. In the world you have tribulation, but take courage; I have overcome the world"* (John 16:33).

As much as I pray that you'll find a therapy that will help you fight your cancer, I'm not simply trying to help you find the right cancer treatment that allows you to have a few more years on this earth. I'd like to help you discover God's cure for eternal separation from Him and the promise of eternal life by receiving Jesus Christ as Savior and Lord. Jesus meant exactly what He said. He *has* overcome the world, and that *is* the right treatment for you and me.

"As we focus on the grace of God, on His character, we can say instead, 'God is loving, and therefore He can bring good out of this situation.'"[1]

NOTE

1. Penelope Stokes (*Grace Under Pressure*, Navpress 1990).

chapter four
The Role of Nutrition in Good Health

Mark Twain once wrote, "A habit cannot be tossed out the window; it must be coaxed down the stairs a step at a time."

Before I had cancer, I thought I was on a reasonably good nutritional plan. Since heart disease was prevalent in my family, I ate a reduced-fat diet and tried to watch my cholesterol. In fact, I may have lowered my cholesterol too much.

In 1990 I had a silent heart attack and never knew that I'd had one. I felt like I had the flu, but the symptoms persisted for more than two weeks, so I went to see my regular physician. And, based on my family history, I took his recommendation to see a cardiologist.

When I stepped on the cardiologist's treadmill, he

asked, "Why didn't you tell me that you've had a lower branch bundle block?"

Surprised, I replied, "I have no idea what you're talking about!"

The doctor stopped the treadmill and said, "Step off the machine. Apparently you've had a heart attack that has destroyed the nerves in the lower part of your heart."

He sent me to a cardiac clinic for a catherization, and they confirmed that my lower anterior descending artery, the one that connects to the bottom of the heart, had about 95 percent blockage. An *angioplasty* (a technique used to open diseased arterial blockage) was performed, and I went on a very stringent diet to further reduce my cholesterol. I was able to bring my cholesterol level down from about 240 to around 100, and I kept it there for seven years.

It really was not until after I was diagnosed with cancer that, looking back on it, I realized that my cholesterol levels might have been too low. But, again, no doctor I talked to during that seven-year period considered that cholesterol levels could be *too* low.

I have since found out that cholesterol plays a major role in the health of your body. Besides just clogging arteries, it has other uses that are very important.

You Really Are What You Eat

My basic diet after the angioplasty became the white meat of chicken, a little fish, and very little red meat—maybe a hamburger once every couple of weeks or so. Beyond that I had no specific nutritional habits. I usually walked three to five miles a day, lived with far too much daily stress (who doesn't?), and generally thought I was in pretty good health. I felt as if I didn't have any troubles—that is, until I took up golf and felt that excruciating pain in my left shoulder.

After I went through the surgeries that I have previously described, I was determined to find out whether my body had the right nutritional levels of vitamins and minerals.

I went to a nutritionist in Atlanta and also consulted with a friend who is a physician and nutritional specialist in Kentucky. I was doing my own double testing, because I wanted to have an M.D. in charge of what I was doing. However, because Kentucky was a long distance phone call, I used the nutritionist in Atlanta for advice and suggestions and then double-checked everything with my friend in Kentucky.

After going through a thorough evaluation that included hair, blood, urine, and saliva analyses, both sets of tests showed fairly significant deficiencies in basic minerals and vitamins and also detected some heavy metals present in my system—beyond what would be considered the norm. Those metals included lead, mercury, and a few other minor ones that I had not heard of before.

The current thinking among nutritionists at that time (perhaps it still is) was that mercury poisoning came primarily from the amalgam (metal alloy) fillings that dentists have used for so long. I suspected that might be true. However, I know my dentist still uses them, along with ceramics and other materials. It seems strange to me that after a tooth is filled with amalgam the dentist places the residual amalgam in a container marked "BIOHAZARDOUS MATERIALS— DO NOT HANDLE."

Think of it: Dentists wear gloves to protect themselves; they put a hazardous (to a degree) material in the mouths of patients who will live with it the rest of their lives; then they place the residual amount of what they don't use in a biohazardous container with a significant warning on its side. That should give us reason to reconsider what we're doing.

To demonstrate the presence of mercury in my mouth, my friend ran a test on me. First he had me brush my teeth. He then took a mercury vapor tester and put it in my mouth. It sampled the ambient level of mercury vapor in my mouth. He then gave me a stick of gum and asked me to chew it for about three minutes. After I had chewed the gum, he remeasured the mercury vapor in my mouth. The levels were more than 10 times what they had been before chewing.

The logical conclusion that he and I drew was that, in the process of chewing, the amalgam fillings in my mouth released small amounts of mercury vapor. Now, whether that has any significant impact on the average person's health or plays any noteworthy role in causing cancer has not been established. But I decided I wouldn't take the chance.

Kidney cancer is not generally thought to be hereditary; therefore, it is very unlikely that I inherited a genetic predisposition to it. Without a doubt, I acquired the cancer somewhere along the way. Did I acquire it from the mercury? Hard to tell, but probably not. However, those amalgam fillings represented something I could change fairly simply, so I did.

Over the next several months I went through the process of having all my amalgam fillings removed and replaced with ceramics. After that, I went back to my friend in order to be tested again for mercury levels and found almost zero ambient mercury levels in my mouth; and after chewing gum it didn't change at all.

I believe in changing what you can change and trying not to worry about those things you can't change. You'll have to draw your own conclusions about whether or not mercury fillings are a health risk.

Cleanse Your Temple

In the New Testament, the apostle Paul wrote to the church at Corinth and explained the following to them.

> "All things are lawful for me, but not all things are profitable . . . I will not be mastered by anything. Food is for the stomach and the stomach is for food, but God will do away with both of them. Yet the body is not for immorality, but for the Lord, and the Lord is for the body. . . . Do you not know that your body is a temple of the Holy Spirit who is in you, whom you have from God, and that you are not your own?" (1 Corinthians 6:12–13, 19).

Because excessive levels of both mercury and lead had been found in my system, I went through a significant routine to cleanse my body of these metals. Because both of these metals tend to accumulate in fatty tissue and don't easily liberate themselves back into the body's system, that is no small task.

To repeat, whether any of these heavy metals have any affect on cancer has not been proved, but the amounts we are exposed to in our daily routines are not normal. We can be exposed to various compounds in the things we eat and the water we drink or even from the soil on which we walk.

I decided to try my best to clear my temple/body of

any and all toxic materials. The process took me the better part of 10 months, but I was able to cleanse my system of the most detectable metals. Interestingly enough, I found the protocol I used in a Harvard Medical School study—not exactly a bastion of alternative treatments.

The method involves the use of large amounts of chlorophyll—that's right, the green stuff that plants use to convert sunlight into sugar. Apparently chlorophyll has a cleansing effect on organic tissues and causes body tissues to liberate many of the toxins that have been stored there, including heavy metals.

You can buy nutritional-quality chlorophyll at any health food store under the name of Chlorella. I went on a regimen, beginning with low doses of chlorophyll and working my way up. My goal was 12 grams of chlorophyll per day, and I ingested that level for about 10 months. At the end of that time, the heavy metals were essentially gone from my body, since they could no longer be detected in my blood, urine, saliva, or hair.

Interestingly, your hair is an indicator of what you are and what you have been, because it seems to store a history of your body's nutritional levels while the hair was growing. For a long time my hair showed traces of mercury and lead. Then, after about 10 months or so, the heavy metals cleared up and haven't been detected in my system since.

Whom Do I Ask?

You might be wondering where to find a nutritionist or an M.D. who understands nutrition well enough to discuss it. In the Appendix of this book you'll find some references to books by doctors who specialize in this area, and I heartily recommend them.

At least two doctors have published books on the subject. Instead of visiting them, it's a whole lot cheaper to buy their books and consider the appropriate recommendations.

I personally prefer reading the books. After all, seeing doctors is expensive and time consuming, especially if they live in another area. So, as far as possible, I try to learn what they know from what they've written. I encourage you to do this as part of your personal nutritional routine.

Basically, you may need to change many of your nutritional habits (or lack thereof). I found I was deficient in four essential minerals and deficient in some important enzymes. Enzymes provide the means of breaking down the essential foods for your body.

According to what I understand, it is virtually useless to take supplements like vitamins and minerals that are relatively expensive if, in fact, enzymes are not also taken. Unless the essential enzymes are present in sufficient quantities, the minerals and vitamins will not break down in the body; they will simply pass right through. Thus, you simply took an expensive laxative.

Let me emphasize that I'm not writing a book on nutrition. There are many very good books on nutrition available, and I encourage you to read some and weigh them in light of your situation. Bear in mind that, as with this book, probably only 80 percent of the information may be applicable to you. It's up to you to separate the facts from the personal opinion information.

You Eat What?

I made several other significant changes in my diet. Again, please understand that I don't consider myself a nutritional expert and don't want to imply that I am. Nevertheless, I did my own research and was a little unnerved with some of the things I discovered.

I live in Hall County, Georgia—one of the largest chicken-growing areas in the entire country. Millions of chickens are raised and slaughtered here every month. Let me tell you a true story that you'll have to take on the basis of my word.

I interviewed five of the largest chicken growers in our area and asked what they feed their chickens and how they raise them. If you had heard their responses firsthand, I suspect you would never eat another processed chicken in your life.

The concluding factor for me was that all five chicken growers said basically the same thing: They never eat the chickens that they raise in their own chicken houses. They do eat chicken but only those that are raised on free-range farms—chickens that have not been fed antibiotics and hormones and are raised naturally, like chickens used to be. Any feed they give their yard chickens contains no antibiotics, hormones, or arsenic to make them hungry.

My personal conclusion was that I would avoid commercially processed chickens. Eating these chickens may have had no adverse effect on me and no effect on the cancer, but it is one of those things I could change and I have.

As a side note, I casually mentioned to one of these chicken growers that now that I've decided not to eat chickens I'd just have to start eating beef again. He smiled and asked me what I thought the chicken growers did with much of their chicken manure these days. He went on to explain that he sold much of the excretion to cattlemen who use it in feedlots as a source of protein for the cattle.

Yes, that's right. The refuse taken from chickens that the poultry farmer won't eat is processed and fed to cows that he won't eat either. He told me that he eats only beef that comes from cows he raises.

Not on My Plate

As you might imagine, I have altered the list of things I will not eat: no chicken or beef unless they were raised by somebody I know and even then very little red meat, because it stays in your system longer than white meats or vegetables. Consequently, whatever additives may be in red meat have a greater chance of being absorbed by your system.

Again, let me make this very clear: I don't know whether these things I've mentioned have had any significant effect on me or the cancer. I can only change the things I can change and not worry about the other things. To me, not eating red meat has not been a big deal.

As long as I'm probably not making friends in the meat-packing business anyway, I might as well tell you that I don't eat pork or veal either; nor do I eat shallow-water fish or shell fish. Occasionally, I do eat deep-water white fish. However, since so much of our inland and coastal waters contain those heavy metals that I've spent so much time and money trying to get out of my system, I choose not to risk absorbing them again by eating foods that contain them.

Occasionally I do eat turkey. I discovered that growers do not raise turkeys in cages the same way they raise chickens, because often they'll die. I do limit my diet to turkeys that are free-range birds and are free of antibiotics and hormones.

Also, another thing I've changed as a result of what I've learned from my reading is the water I drink. I don't drink tap water any more. Let me clarify that. I don't think there's anything especially wrong with the tap water in America; it's certainly better than most places in the world. However, we add lots of different chemicals, such as chlorine (to kill bacteria) and fluoride (for fighting tooth decay).

Again, I'm not sure that's bad for me or that it has an impact on my cancer, but it's one of those things I can change. I drink only double-filtered, ozonated water. Ozonating the water kills bacteria without using chemicals.

I choose bottled water when I travel, and we have a whole-house filtering system at home. I've been drinking filtered and ozonated water for eight years and, during that time, I have significantly increased the volume of water I drink. I do that primarily because I have only one kidney and I don't want to lose it. Instead, I want to help that remaining kidney do its work. My daily consumption of water is about one ounce of water for every pound I weigh—and that's a lot of water. Don't be scared off by the math on that one. Believe me, it takes a long time to get used to drinking that much water, but you can do it.

It probably would be better for me to eat organic foods and raw vegetables, but because of my travel schedule I haven't been able to do that. Also, organically grown vegetables and fruits are very expensive. However, although I don't eat organic foods, I try to carefully choose the companies that provide the foods I buy or else get them from local farmers who don't use a lot of pesticides and chemicals on their crops. Large companies can afford the chemical and pesticide treatments, but I've found that all those chemicals are too expensive for many small local growers.

I like to eat raw vegetables—carrots, celery, cucumbers, and others—but for me it would be impossible to eat all my vegetables raw. I eat a lot of salads when I travel, and although that may sound like a good thing there may be chemical pollutants in those vegetables at the salad bar, so I still have to be careful not to eat too much of them—particularly the root vegetables that absorb so many chemicals from the ground. This is a plan that works for me. Remember that you must do what you can do for yourself.

I regularly check my system to see if I'm getting sufficient amounts of minerals, vitamins, and protein. If I were to choose not to eat any meat at all, I'd have to increase my intake of protein some other way, such as by eating vegetable-based protein.

Your Plate, Your Choice

Of course, I'll admit that if I were to stay on a very stringent, healthy diet, it probably would be better for me. Any true nutritionist will probably shudder about now when I admit that

I periodically eat French fries or some other junk foods. I just don't eat them regularly and don't eat a lot of them when I do.

Perhaps I could be healthier by staying on a strict vegetarian diet, but I've just found that I can't do that and, therefore, I don't.

As a Christian I also keep in mind that, in terms of food, the apostle Peter was told by the Lord in his vision to *"kill and eat."* Peter, being a Jew, found this to be a very difficult command from God.

Peter said, *"I saw the four-footed animals of the earth and the wild beasts and the crawling creatures and the birds of the air. I also heard a voice saying to me, 'Get up, Peter; kill and eat.' But I said, 'By no means, Lord, for nothing unholy or unclean has ever entered my mouth.' But a voice from heaven answered a second time, 'What God has cleansed, no longer consider unholy'"* (Acts 11:5–9).

If you read the dietary law in the Old Testament, you'll see that those rules were pretty stringent. If you'll read Leviticus 11:1–23 and Deuteronomy 14:1–21, you'll find the laws were pretty inflexible. But God told the apostle Peter that nothing is unclean that has been created by Him; therefore, it was all right to kill and eat. (See Acts 10:9–16.)

In other words, I think all foods were made by God potentially for man to eat. However, I also remember that the apostle Paul said, *"All things are lawful, but not all things are profitable. All things are lawful, but not all things edify"* (1 Corinthians 10:23).

From a biblical perspective I could probably eat a buzzard if I wanted to. I don't think it would taste very good or be very nutritious; therefore, I've never been tempted to eat a buzzard.

All things are potential food for us, because as Christians there's no prohibition against eating whatever we want. However, there are some things that aren't particularly good for us, and we should try to avoid those things. That's what I do.

Nutrition and You

Let me also say, I believe that very few M.D.s really understand the role of good nutrition and health. Primarily, doctors have a tendency to discount the healing effects of good nutrition, because it's been used in some strange circles for a long time. Let me explain what I mean.

Several years ago I had a friend who was really into nutrition. Her husband was a doctor and she was a very knowledgeable. One day I went with her to make a run to the health food store. As we were walking through the store I said, "Margaret, look around here. What do you see?"

She stopped and, with a puzzled look on her face, took a look around. Suddenly she laughed, because the only other clients in the store were hippies. The store had been carrying health food for the hippie generation for a long time, and some of them were pretty fanatical about it. In fact, I find that when I talk to health-food purists from the sixties, they're still fanatical about eating only seeds, berries, and nuts. I try to point out to my more radical friends that one of their heroes, Euell Gibbons, ate only nuts, berries, and pinecones, and he died of cancer. I suppose one of the reasons health foods have gotten a somewhat dubious reputation is because of the fervor of the hippies.

However, many of these health foods are very good for us. So I recommend that physicians learn something about nutrition and the role of so-called health foods. Books written by some of the qualified physicians are referenced in the Appendix.

Nutrition plays a vital role in the health of our bodies. And its not simply a matter of the foods we eat; it's the other things we consume along with the food—enzymes, proteins, and other necessary nutrients we need to absorb the foods and derive their maximum benefits.

Actually, it amazes me that many doctors have discounted the impact of nutrition in the area of medicine. Nutrition is an area of medicine. Think, for example, how scurvy was cured. It was done through nutrition.

Many diseases that were once virtually eradicated are

actually beginning to show up again, because of a lack of emphasis on proper nutrition. Nutrition plays an important role in our health and may play an absolutely vital role in the area of dealing with cancer. I can't prove that, but I believe future studies will validate it. First we must eradicate the exaggerations on the part of nutritional enthusiasts, and then we need to eliminate the preconceived biases of many in the medical profession.

Sugar Is Poison

One of the things I've learned about cancer is that it lives on sugars. In fact, one of the tests for cancer (PET scan) uses sugar with a radioactive tag in it to detect cancer, because cancer assimilates sugar so readily. So try to avoid as much sugar as possible. Cancer readily metabolizes sugar; it does not readily metabolize fat.

Watch Out for Aliens

I've shared with you the little I know about nutrition. I've spoken with many good nutritionists and learned much from them. When I speak at conferences, people often ask me questions about nutrition, and I always tell them the same thing: I am not a nutritionist and certainly don't consider myself an expert. I am a cancer patient who is trying to stay alive, and I am convinced that good nutrition helps me do that.

Therefore, to the best of my ability, I eat as healthy as I can. I encourage you to do the same, especially if you're raising children. Americans are fat people, because they eat too much fat, too many carbohydrates, and especially too much sugar. Unfortunately, we are accelerating the health crisis in America by cramming our kids with too much junk food.

I have my own personal theory about this (and I trust you know that this is facetious). In 1947 it was thought that flying saucers and aliens from outer space visited the earth. It is my theory that the aliens established all of the fast-food restaurants in America that we now see. And they did it to fatten up Americans so that when they return they'll have a good food supply.

If you don't believe that, just travel the world. Almost everybody outside of our country is thin. Americans are fat people, and when the aliens return they'll begin their search for fat people. So if you want to avoid being eaten by an alien, my advice is to stay out of fast-food restaurants.

Be Persistent in Your Efforts

Henry Ward Beecher said, "The difference between perseverance and obstinacy is that one comes from a strong will and the other from a strong won't." It's up to you.

chapter five
The Role of Alternative Medicine

Over the last seven years I have confirmed that not every alternative medicine is good, and not every alternative medicine is bad. Nevertheless, that seems to be the way the sides are developing right now. It's a binary decision: "Yes, I like it," or "No, I don't like it," and that's never the best way to make a choice.

Essentially, alternative medicine is a supplement to traditional medicine. Many of the treatments used by alternative therapists predate the so-called traditional therapies by several hundred years. That alone does not impute validity, but no therapy would survive hundreds of years and millions of users without some significant effectiveness.

The negative side of many good alternative therapies is that they cannot be patented; thus, there is little profit to be made. If the traditional medicines being used were cures, and we knew that when we went to our doctors we would be restored to health and never have to face cancer again, there'd be no need for alternative medicines, except perhaps as preventatives to getting cancer in the first place.

Perhaps that's the way medicine will be one day. We may be able to modify cancer genetically or find a vaccine or something else that will cure or prevent cancer and it will solve the majority of our problems. I believe that when we do it will be a blend of the therapies we now call traditional and alternative.

However, as long as traditional medicine has the high failure rates we now see, using systemic poisons and tissue-killing radiation, people will look for alternatives. Chemotherapy may be the best available cancer treatment in most hospitals, but it is not good enough. Just ask most chemo patients.

Learning from Others

Because of what I do for a living (teaching and counseling), I've known a lot of physicians. I've also gotten to know many physicians in an obviously different relationship: as a cancer patient. I also know a lot of alternative medicine practitioners. Some are M.D.s, some Ph.D.s, and others have degrees they just made up.

Speaking very candidly, I have to say that most of the alternative medicine practitioners that I've met are a little unusual. They often are very single-minded and defensive about their trade, and sometimes they ignore good science as a result.

Many alternative medicine practitioners have hurt themselves, because they boast of academic degrees they don't have and, in many instances, the degrees are fabricated. That hurts their cause. In my opinion, they'd be far better off to represent themselves as laypersons who have a lot of specific knowledge and are teaching on a particular topic and simply let it go at that, unless they have earned degrees in some scientific area.

Nobody Is Perfect

I have concluded that you should never listen to more than about 75 percent of what most alternative practitioners teach and do. I've learned that lesson the hard way.

Originally, when I met an alternative practitioner (most of those I've used have earned M.D. degrees), if that person suggested something I considered weird, I had a tendency to totally discount that individual. I also found that to be an error. Just as in traditional medicine, you'll find that doctors focus on a particular therapy and are likely to want to treat everybody the same way.

My friend Dr. Larry Hyde (an ob-gyn) said that when

his group discovered hysterectomies it wasn't long before every woman *needed* a hysterectomy. Or once urologists discovered prostatectomies, pretty soon every man with prostate cancer had to have his prostate removed. You get the picture.

Obviously, this is not true with every doctor, but the tendency to overapply successful therapies is common. This sort of thing is true both in traditional medicine and alternative medicine. Doctors find something they like, or something comes along that's new and exciting because it helps someone, and the propensity is to apply it to everybody.

I have had alternative therapists try to do that with me. The "cures" have ranged all the way from colonics (a pretty awful thing to go through) to kinetics and kinesiology (a system originating in the chiropractic profession that uses muscle testing to evaluate health problems). And there are lots of other alternative treatments, ranging from bean sprouts to beetle nuts. Perhaps some of these treatments do work for some people, but they seem a bit bizarre to me.

I had an alternative medicine doctor who was convinced that the proper alignment of the earth's magnetic lines of force would make a significant difference in my health. In other words, the direction in which my bed was aligned, relative to the North Pole, was important. To prove it to me he used a couple of copper divining rods. Now, I still don't know what copper rods (a nonmagnetic mineral) have to do with magnetic lines of force, but he certainly believed in it. I concluded that it was nonsense, and as a result I was tempted to discount everything he said.

I'll have to admit that over the years I've found this decision policy can be a bad philosophy. Just because someone says one thing that seems a little strange, that certainly doesn't mean that everything he or she does or says is worthless. Don't miss learning from others.

Variations on the Theme

Many practicing medical doctors also use alternative medicines. They may or may not broadcast it, but M.D.s are involved with vitamin therapy, ozone therapy, unique radiation therapies, and many other kinds of alternative treatments. That doesn't make them wrong; it just means you need to be discerning.

Some of the traditional medical doctors I've met are superior people, and some of the alternative medicine doctors are also superior. I think of men like Dr. Jim McCoy, the molecular biologist who died while he was developing a cancer vaccine; or the cancer specialist from Helsinki, Finland, Dr. Thomas Tallberg, who has compiled the most exhaustive record on cancer therapies of anybody I have ever seen. Then there are others like Dr. Roy Page, who uses radiation therapy in a unique way to help his patients, and Dr.

Patrick Sewell, who uses cryogenic ablation to help kill cancer tumors, rather than remove them surgically.

I'm sure there are many others, but I mention these men because I have personally benefited from their talents and expertise. These are not weird people. Some of the things they do may seem a bit unusual right now, but it's only because we're not accustomed to their unique methods. These are highly skilled scientists who think outside the box; just as Alexander Graham Bell, Madame Curie, Jonas Salk, and countless others have over the centuries.

How many doctors have you ever met who, instead of surgically removing a tumor from your body, would stick a needle into the tumor and freeze it? That's a little bit unusual, but you know what? I believe that in another decade the method that Dr. Sewell has perfected will become common therapy for anybody with early cancer detection. What seems unorthodox today may become traditional treatment tomorrow.

Citrus Fruits and Milk

Do you recall what I said earlier about scurvy? It is perhaps the oldest known deficiency disease, yet its cause was not recognized until the 20th century. Scurvy is caused by lack of vitamin C—ascorbic acid—and it was very common among seamen on long voyages, because of their inadequate consumption of fresh fruits and vegetables. The cure for scurvy is an "alternative treatment": simply eat fruits and vegetables that are high in vitamin C content.

Rickets is another disorder that responds to an alternative treatment. Rickets can produce skeletal problems, such as bowlegs and spinal and dental deformities, and is caused primarily due to a lack of sunlight and vitamin D, or a lack of calcium or phosphates. The alternative therapy treatment for rickets is to maintain an adequate intake of calcium, phosphorus, and vitamin D, which are found in milk.

Neither of these diseases are corrected by cutting something out or by prescribing a patented drug. The same can be said of smallpox and polio vaccines. At the time these vaccines were developed, they were alternative medicines; and, to the medical community, they were strange.

It took a long time to convince the medical profession that these treatments were legitimate. Not until smallpox and polio were eliminated in our country were doctors totally convinced that those therapies were "acceptable." Then they became traditional therapies.

Let me say something as kindly as I can: I believe that licensed M.D.s who prescribe chemical poisons and potentially lethal doses of radiation to treat cancer should be a lot more tolerant of alternative medicine than many of them are.

I understand the philosophy behind chemotherapy

and radiation, and it does work for some people. And, in many cases, it may be the only treatment available for some cancers. However, think about it: Isn't it just a little peculiar to go into a doctor's office with cancer, which may already be making you feel bad, and then have a doctor prescribe a systemic poison that he asserts will help you get over your disease?

In 100 years, people will probably look back at our traditional therapies—removing body parts, poisoning people with chemicals, and burning out parts with radiation—and think, *how bizarre*—just like we now think about doctors who used to bleed people to cure them.

The Fine Line of Truth

I don't mean this in a condescending way, but I have talked to many practicing physicians who believe that all alternative therapies are worthless, regardless of where they come from or the qualifications of the doctors administering the therapies. That's unfortunate and quite narrow-minded. Just because an alternative medicine does not meet all the standards established by the FDA, who's to say our standards are correct? Are our principles/values more profit motivated than they are people oriented?

I am bothered with allergies, and recently I watched a TV news program about allergies. The program noted that a doctor in France has developed drops that are given orally, as opposed to taking allergy shots. One of my grandsons is going through a series of allergy shots right now, so I perked up when I heard that.

At the conclusion of the TV presentation, a practicing American allergist said he would not accept this therapy, because it has not been proved to his satisfaction. He wanted exhaustive clinical studies done, using both shots and sublingual drops, to determine which application was more effective.

Keep in mind that this medical treatment has been used by medical doctors in France on more than one million people. They certainly have adequate data to determine if it works. It has helped, not hurt, one million people. Doesn't it seem much more logical to allow American patients to make the choice? If, at the end of some predetermined time the patients weren't better, they could always return to the shots. Unfortunately, if the alternative treatments don't meet our standards, too often we assume they're no good.

In order to get sublingual drops in the United States, it's almost certain that exhaustive clinical tests will be required, several hundred million dollars well be spent in the process, and the cost of the drugs will be prohibitively expensive to the majority of people who need them. Somehow, that doesn't make a lot of sense to me.

Again, I believe that traditional doctors should learn to lower their biases a bit and learn to become a little more tolerant. That doesn't mean they have to accept everything blindly; some of it *is* worthless, but don't discard the useful with the useless.

Nothing New Under the Sun

Most nutritionists today practice alternative medicine. I have a good friend who has been diagnosed with chronic fatigue syndrome. My friend has spent in excess of $100,000 trying to treat this very debilitating disease. He's a very active person, but because of chronic fatigue he is virtually nonfunctional at times and becomes very depressed.

The nutritionist he goes to has seen many cases of chronic fatigue syndrome and believes the disease is linked to high doses of antibiotics. People who have received antibiotics in high or too-frequent doses basically kill not only the bad bacteria but also the good bacteria in their systems. Then, when they stop taking the antibiotics, *candida* (a yeast infection that begins in the digestive system and spreads to other parts of the body) expands uncontrollably. The nutritionist believes this very high level of yeast infection is what produces chronic fatigue syndrome.

In alternative medicine, nutritionists are taught that when someone stops taking antibiotics, to reload the intestines with the right bacteria, that person should be given heavy doses of acidophilus or bidophilus.

This is not a marvelous new treatment that has just been developed. Veterinarians have been using this on pigs for decades. After swine take high doses of antibiotics they get sick, so veterinarians have found that giving preventative doses of acidophilus keep the swine from becoming sicker.

So, why haven't we transferred this brilliant technology over to human beings? Because it hasn't been proved clinically. As a result, we have hundreds of thousands—perhaps millions—of people suffering from chronic fatigue syndrome, or other post-antibiotic symptoms, who probably wouldn't have to.

Another example of alternative medicine that has now become traditional therapy comes from veterinary science. Swine generally catch many of the same diseases that human beings do, and for this reason they are used for experimentation, because of the similarity to human systems.

For instance, pigs get ulcers just like humans do. For decades, humans with ulcers were treated with a bland diet and heavy doses of antacids. Then, if they didn't get better or they developed bleeding ulcers, the person was cut open, repaired, and sewn back up. This proved to be an ineffective way to treat ulcers, because they had a tendency to reappear. Also, surgery was a very costly treatment and very wearing on the patient.

But when a pig had an ulcer, the veterinarian would give the pig a combination of antibiotics and bismol (as in Pepto-Bismol). And guess what? It cured their ulcers. Veterinarians have known for a long time that bacteria causes most ulcers, not food or stomach acid.

Consequently, now humans are taking the same treatment swine have been taking for decades. And it's no longer alternative medicine; it's traditional medicine.

Not Everything That Comes Along

The point I'm trying to emphasize is that we need to be a little more tolerant of alternative medicines. Of course, to determine whether they work or don't work, we should hold them to legitimate standards. But it doesn't necessarily mean that all alternative medicines and treatments have to be held to the same clinical standards that we require with the potentially life-threatening chemicals (we call medicines) that we take.

Again, just because there may some strange, creative people involved with alternative medicines, that doesn't necessarily make the people or the treatments bad.

But there's a danger in going the other way. Some people have never seen an alternative therapy they didn't like and would probably try them all, and then they'd tell everyone they knew that they should try them too. To some alternative advocates it doesn't even matter if you're in perfect health; take it anyway.

The suggested therapies for my cancer have included coffee enemas, colonics, and something that's been used for years in mining communities to extract lead from miners' systems: chelation therapy.

Chelation therapy, a series of intravenous infusions, seems to be making its way throughout the alternative medicine community as a way to cleanse arterial plaque, reduce harmful free radicals, remove heavy metals, increase blood flow, strengthen blood vessels and veins, and generally perform as a cure-all for just about everything from heart disease to cancer. And that's with absolutely no verifiable data to support this belief—at least none I have found.

One of the things I've found with many practitioners involved in alternative therapies is that they tend to treat nonexistent diseases and toxic conditions and then tell you that they have cured the disease or toxic condition that didn't exist in the first place.

I have a couple of personal examples. My wife and I were going through an evaluation with some alternative practitioners in another state. Through the art of kinesiology (determining how your muscles react to a particular stimulant), Judy was diagnosed as having a chronic infection in her jawbone, which was suspected to be the source of all her ills. Interestingly enough, I was also diagnosed with the same ailment. This practitioner told me that it was probably the original cause of my cancer.

Well, by that time I had learned to discount about 20 percent of what most people say and 100 percent of what some people say. I wasn't particularly impressed that this individual had enough knowledge in the field of diagnostic medicine for me to go to a dentist and allow my jaw to be cut open to see if I had a problem.

Unfortunately my wife was much more willing to take his advice, and we went to see the dentist he recommended. Sure enough, the dentist told Judy that she had an infection in her jawbone that was causing a lot of the symptoms she was experiencing. Later we learned that most of the symptoms she was experiencing were caused by a degenerative vertebrae in her lower back.

Unfortunately, Judy was very receptive to what the dentist had to say. I tried my best to talk her out of allowing him to cut into her jaw, but she let him do it. He scraped the bone and supposedly solved her alleged problem (that I wasn't convinced even existed). As a result, she now has nerve damage in her jaw that has bothered her for the last several years. I really regret not talking her out of having that done.

I wouldn't allow them to do the same treatment on me. We returned home and I went to see a good friend who is an oral surgeon and described the diagnosis to him. To his credit, he didn't discount what the other dentist had said; he just said he was skeptical about it. However, he added that if the level of infection that the other doctor described existed in my jawbone he should have been able to pick it up in an X ray, and he didn't. I appreciated that, because it verified my skepticism.

However, I then asked if he would be willing to make two incisions, one on either side of my jaw, and look inside to see if I did have the problem that had been described. After all, I do have cancer, I was looking for answers, and I thought this might be a reasonable and non-debilitating solution.

After a short pause, my friend looked at me and said, "I probably wouldn't do this for anybody else, but because you are looking for answers I'll do it for you."

He made the incisions and looked inside my jawbone. Guess what? No infection and no problems of any kind. If I had allowed the other dentist to do it, I'm sure he would have announced that he had found a problem inside. And I'm just as sure that he would have said that he had cured it for me.

The moral of the story: Be extremely careful in your pursuit of alternative medicines. Don't let anyone diagnose you with a nonexistent disease, treat you with a strange remedy, and then tell you they have cured you from something you didn't have. You have no certain way to know what you're getting into, so be very careful.

Reasons I'm Alive Today

"One of the most difficult challenges in living is knowing when to act and when to wait. . . . The full-time vocation of living is to seek and know the Lord and His will and act on His timing, strategy, and power."[1]

The more serious the illness, the more important it is for you to fight back, mobilizing all your resources—spiritual, emotional, intellectual, physical.

Although the cancer I have normally kills more than 90 percent of the people who have it within two to three years, I believe that I am alive today for three reasons.

First and foremost, I'm alive because of the prayers of God's people. I believe that God has interceded on my behalf as His people prayed. Does that mean He has cured me? I haven't asked Him to, but I'm still here—still alive and still feeling well. To me that's a touch of God's grace.

The second reason I'm here and still alive is because I was able to get good alternative therapies to help boost my immune system early on and fight off secondary diseases, as well as fighting off the cancer to the highest degree possible.

The third reason I believe I'm still here is because of traditional medicine. I have received the best traditional medicine that America has to offer, both in surgery and in wise counsel from physicians.

Because traditional medicine didn't offer me much in terms of long-term therapy for my particular disease, I had to go elsewhere. That doesn't mean that traditional medicine is bogus or that cures are being kept off the market. It simply means that traditional medicine hasn't yet found the cure for my particular cancer.

How I Screen Alternative Therapies

Let me share the criteria I have established for myself and that I try to live by when evaluating any therapies, alternative or otherwise.

Discernment: If I am going to review or use a therapy, I want it to be administered or controlled by a licensed physician if at all possible. The practitioner must have an earned degree in the science that person is applying. In other words, just because a person has a Ph.D. in mechanical engineering doesn't mean he or she is an expert in cancer, any more than someone with a Ph.D. in nutrition is an expert in building bridges. So, be very discerning.

Open-minded to breakthroughs: I look for treatments that will help my problem or treatments that have been helpful for diseases similar to mine. As I said before, I've been told the only cancer that is similar to renal cell carcinoma is melanoma. So, I often look for treatments for melanoma that might potentially help solve my problem.

Of course, if I hear something about a breakthrough in another disease—like breast cancer or colon cancer—I'll take a look at that too. I then try to find someone who is an expert in renal cell cancer, share what I have learned, and ask if that person thinks the new breakthrough might help me.

I've done that many times. In the majority of cases the answer comes back negative, because it isn't applicable to my problem. Nevertheless, perhaps one day soon somebody will be able to modify a new therapy and make it applicable to my disease. It never hurts anyone to keep an open mind.

Verifiable statistics: I want the best data available on the treatments I try. That includes both therapies and supplements.

I presently take two supplements that are sold through a multilevel system. I don't discount them because of their marketing plan. I have a good friend in a research lab, and I've sent him lots of products to evaluate for me. The ones he recommends are the only ones I try. I've isolated the two I take on a regular basis and they have been very helpful to me.

At this point I hesitate to share the information,

because even though they work for me that doesn't mean they'll work for you too. However, I'm going to do it anyway, because this book is really my personal testimony.

I take a product called Juice Plus; you'll find a reference to it in the Appendix. Both a fruit and a vegetable supplement are offered, but I take only the fruit. I find that it helps my energy level. It contains live enzymes, which I believe are essential.

In addition, I take a product called Co-Enzyme Q-10, which is basically an antioxidant. I take this primarily because my friend in the lab believes it to be a very effective compound, specifically for people with cancer. As we get older, our bodies manufacture less and less of the enzyme it takes to stay healthy, which is found in Co-Enzyme Q-10. Those are the two most important supplements I take to try to stay healthy. You may find other sources and other products that work for you. These just happen to work well for me.

I also use a water-filtering system in my home, marketed by the company that provides Juice Plus. I use it for a couple of reasons. Although I drink filtered and ozonated water, it's much too expensive for everybody in my family to drink, so it's cheaper for us to filter our own water. Also, the water in our homes contains chlorine, and a person can absorb chlorine while showering about as readily as when drinking the water. I wanted to take both the chlorine and the fluoride out of the water I use to shower.

Again, I understand that it may make no difference at all to my cancer. However, it's one of those things I *can* do, and it's a change recommended by several specialists I respect. So I do it. I think it works for me. It may not work for you. You'll have to decide for yourself.

Verifiable therapies: I select alternative therapies I use based on the evidence that they will not do me any further harm. In other words, I don't want to take a therapy that's going to further injure my body, suppress my immune system, or give the cancer a better-than-even chance to kill me.

I try to avoid debilitating therapies if possible, and it takes a lot of research to determine what's harmful and what's not. It also requires a lot of discussion with people who have knowledge in this area.

Generally, I'm not willing to be the first person to take a therapy. I realize that someone has to be first. However, some of those who are first may not survive, and I would rather take only therapies that have been well evaluated. Again, I have that luxury, because I am still in excellent health.

Reasonable cost: I'm not poor, but neither do I have unlimited funds. Most alternative therapies will not be covered by insurance, so you'll have to bear the cost yourself. The cost has to be what I can afford, because I don't want to ask somebody else to pay for the cost of my research.

Obviously, God can provide the funds from many places, and I know that many people I've talked to have received help from family, friends, and churches that have raised money, and that's great. God has not chosen to do that for me, so one of my criteria is reasonable cost. I believe this makes me more discerning.

Nothing bizarre: No weird diagnostic tools can be used in the treatment. I don't want to use kinesiology, because I'm not sure I accept its validity. I don't want electromagnetic testing devices, or dark-background microscopes, or any other strange thing—from tossing chicken bones to reading animal intestines. Let me assure you that I have been contacted by people who use every one of those things in their so-called diagnoses of disease, and I could probably give you another two dozen strange examples.

I recommend that you stay away from them—like I do. You'll have to make your own decisions though.

Independent testing: I want to be able to test the efficacy (the effectiveness of the treatment) by using traditional tests, such as immune system tests, blood tests, and those kinds of things. This criterion is very difficult to apply and has eliminated a lot of alternative therapies.

I want to verify some positive change and not be totally dependent on what somebody tells me is happening. When I tried the vaccine therapy, the electromagnetic therapy, and the mineral and vitamin therapies, I always used a recognized, independent laboratory to test the results.

For the first four or five years of my disease, while I was taking the therapy from Prague in the Czech Republic, I regularly had immune system tests run. I knew where my immune system started out, the effect the compound had on me, and how long it took to wear off.

Those tests were not cheap. Each immune system test cost several hundred dollars, but I felt it was money well spent, particularly because you don't get to make many mistakes with cancer.

I use traditional tests. If you choose to do so, that means you'll have to do some reading to find out what tests are available. There are some very good ones. I use a test called the IL8 test, which is a profile of the entire immune system. With that one test I can tell very quickly whether my immune system is responding to a particular therapy.

It Is Worth Investigating

Alternative therapies are everywhere. Alternative therapy enthusiasts are a little like Christians. Once you get to know one Christian, you'll get to know lots of Christians.

Once you get a little information from one alternative therapist, you may suddenly find yourself overwhelmed with others.

The Internet is my primary resource to find alternative therapies listed for my diseases. My second resource is to talk to family and friends and tell them what I'm looking for. People send me articles from all over the world about new therapies being developed. Or somebody will call and say, "Larry you need to listen to *60 Minutes* tonight; they're doing a thing on cancer." Or, perhaps Larry King will talk to someone who has been cured of cancer. That's where a lot of this kind of information comes from, but it won't come overnight. My opinion is that, for most of us, the Internet is probably the best overall tool for research.

As I said, once you get inside the alternative therapy circle, you'll find articles and magazines on the Internet, and you may even decide to subscribe to one of the magazines or health newsletters. However, I'm not recommending any individuals or magazines. The choice is yours.

Not One or the Other

As I've said before, in my opinion, alternative medicine is a logical adjunct to traditional medicine. It's not a replacement, and it's not an either/or decision; it's an "and" situation.

In my case, the alternative therapies I have chosen

have blended well with traditional, and my primary physician is very helpful. The longer I survive in good health, the more he accepts my eccentricities.

You will have to decide if alternative therapies make sense for you. I have done some things and been some places that made no sense and felt like I had wasted my time and money; however, I was willing to do that in order to learn. You have to decide if you can tolerate that uncertainty.

I have suggested some therapies I thought would help some terminally ill patients that friends asked to call me. A few investigated the options I suggested but most did not. I am constantly amazed at how many people would rather die than switch (their opinions). But it is their choice.

You might be married to someone who thinks alternative medicine is a waste of time and won't help you, so you will have to make your own decision. How far can you go? Or, your physician might say, "If you do that, I'll stop treating you." In my opinion, unless you wholeheartedly agree with him or her, go find yourself another physician, because that one is too closed-minded.

Nobody knows everything, and nobody has the exact answer. If you could walk into your physician's office and he or she could say, "I know exactly what's wrong with you. I'll give you this, and in six months you'll be totally cured and won't ever have this cancer again," that would be terrific.

However, that cure doesn't exist. So both your physician and you need to be open-minded. If he or she is not, you probably need to find someone else.

I've listed some books in the Appendix that were very helpful for me and I hope will be helpful to you.

Let me close this chapter with some words of encouragement. "In the pure strong hours of the morning, when the soul of the day is at its best, lean upon the windowsill of the Lord and look into His face, and get orders for the day. Then go out into the world with a sense of a Hand upon your shoulder and not a chip.[2]

NOTES

1. Lloyd Ogilvie, chaplain of the U.S. Senate.
2. E. Stanley Jones, an extraordinary missionary for over half a century (1884–1972).

chapter six
Peaceful Not Passive

Whence you are in the midst of a crisis, there's a significant difference between being peaceful and being passive. Passivity means suffering through something that possibly you could change by exerting a little effort. God does not want His people to be passive.

Jesus said, *"Peace I leave with you; My peace I give to you; not as the world gives do I give to you. Do not let your heart be troubled, nor let it be fearful"* (John 14:27).

Peace is totally different from passivity. Passivity means we wallow in our pity and think that we're suffering because of some sins we have committed and that God doesn't care any more. That's wrong. That's absolutely untrue.

Peace means that you're actively doing everything you can to change the circumstance you are in, but you refuse to worry. Maybe you can't change what's happening, but you'll never know unless you try. If you can't change the circumstances, then maybe God wants you to learn something through it all. Worry is the result of taking on a responsibility that belongs to God, so be at peace; He's in control.

Leo Tolstoy said, "Where there is faith, there is love; where there is love, there is peace; where there is peace, there is God; and where there is God, there is no need."

Focus on Faith, Not Fear

"As an emotion in and of itself, fear is not wrong; it is often an instinctive response to a perceived threat. But when you choose to remain in a fearful state, allowing the anxiety and tension to mount unchecked, you then move into a position of not trusting God to take care of you."[1]

After my initial diagnosis of cancer in 1995, I experienced the supernatural peace of God. I was driving back from North Carolina as a result of a phone call I received from my physician, who told me that I had a tumor under my left shoulder blade.

It was enlightening to me that my biggest concern at the time was not the tumor. I had no idea at that point whether it was malignant or nonmalignant. Never having experienced cancer before, my biggest concern was whether or not I was going to end up living in fear. Earlier, I had been unaware of the heart attack I'd had, so there was nothing to worry about. By the time I knew about it the heart attack was over.

I did not want to live in fear, because I had seen many Christians who, when faced with a grave crisis like cancer or death, had their faith crumple, and their Christian witness was adversely affected. So, my concern was whether that would happen to me. I think an analogy might be those who have gone into war. I've heard many of them say their biggest fear in battle was that they might turn out to be cowards and run in the face of the enemy. If not managed properly, fear is a crippling, debilitating emotion. In fact, fear closes many doors in our lives that only Christ can open.

Actually, most people discover that fear doesn't last once it's faced. It's then that their inner strength shows up— particularly for Christians. Their faith doesn't get weaker; it becomes stronger. As a result, they don't have to live in fear.

Samuel Johnson, lexicographer and author, wrote, "The cure for the greatest part of human miseries is not radical but palliative [calming]."

I wanted to continue to live with the peace of God that I had in my life, and I believe that God gave me His supernatural peace at the time when I needed it the most. For instance, I recall that I found myself listening almost dispassionately as I heard the doctors explain my CT scans and tell me the statistics about the low survival rate of my particular cancer. It was as if the doctor was explaining someone else's problems.

I truly experienced the supernatural peace of God. I believe that is what God promises His people and, if we just trust Him, He will provide it. I certainly have found that to be true.

The apostle Paul tells us to *"Be anxious for nothing, but in everything by prayer and supplication with thanksgiving let your requests be made known to God. And the peace of God, which surpasses all comprehension, will guard your hearts and your minds in Christ Jesus"* (Philippians 4:6–7).

Think about that. If you or a loved one has cancer, this passage must become real to you. It cannot simply be words on paper.

When Paul said we should not be *anxious,* he used the word *merimnao,* which means the same thing as fearful. In the Greek it means to be of a divided mind, troubled, worried. So we are not to be fearful about anything; instead, we should pray. And that doesn't mean to just send up a request once in awhile. The word *supplication* means that we are to regularly and persistently ask God to give us His peace. The promise of God's Word is that we can have the *"peace of God, which surpasses all comprehension."*

In other words, the circumstances don't have to be reasonable, or even understandable, for us to have God's peace. You don't have to have a cure or be assured that you'll live for a long time in order to have peace from God. If that were true, the peace wouldn't have to come from God; it would simply come as a result of good circumstances.

"True peace is available only in knowing Christ intimately. All that he said, did, and does is to bring peace in our hearts. He was born to bring it; He taught to explain it; His life modeled it; He died on the cross to establish it; He rose from the dead to defeat all the enemies that rob us of it; and He is with each of us now to give the gift. It pervades our hearts when we put Him first in our lives."[2]

The apostle Paul assures us that God's peace *"will guard your hearts and your minds in Christ Jesus,"* and that's very important. That means that the enemy cannot come in and steal our peace and happiness or make us frustrated, miserable, fearful, anxious people. That wouldn't be living anymore. We'd just be hanging around, afraid to die. And that's never been God's plan for His people, trust me.

Do You Really Believe God?

"Worry is atheism if you did not know, for you are saying to God, 'You are not in control.'"[3]

I think that one of the most discouraging things I've seen in my 33 years as a believer has been fearful Christians. By that I mean people who profess to know Jesus Christ and say they believe in Jesus Christ. I think they do believe *in* Christ but they don't really *believe* Christ. That's obvious, because of their fear, frustration, and anxiety.

You see, to believe *in* Christ means that you acknowledge He exists; but to *believe* Christ means you trust Him absolutely, and He is in fact the omnipotent Creator of all that exists. You believe that nothing can happen to you unless God has either ordered it for your life or has allowed it in your life. That doesn't necessarily mean that God caused it, but it does mean that God knows you are able to go through whatever circumstance you face and come out the other side stronger. As a result you'll have a witness to other people.

"There should be a sheer sparkle about the Christian life; and too often the Christian dresses like a mourner at a funeral, and talks like a specter at a feast."[4]

The reason we are here is to be God's witnesses. We are all witnessing all the time about what Christ has or has not done in us. Our mission is not to demonstrate how to live to an old age, make lots of money, and look successful. We're here to demonstrate God's love, peace, and power through us, no matter what the circumstances.

For some people that means cancer; for some it means poverty; and perhaps for some it means wealth, health, and prosperity. In my case, God has chosen to use me to witness to people as a result of the difficulties I'm going through.

I certainly don't intend to compare myself to the apostle Paul, but I believe that what he said about "learning to be content in all things"—whether in plenty or little, good or bad circumstances—is what God wants for His people.

Learn to be content in all things. Remember that fear and worry come from taking on responsibilities that belong to God. Oswald Chambers wrote that "Faith is a deliberate confidence in the character of God whose ways you may not understand at the time."

Single-Mindedness

The kind of peace we're all after comes supernaturally from God, but I believe the key to peace is through a voluntary effort on our part to die to self.

To die to self is to turn your life over to the Lord Jesus Christ. If He decides that it's best for you to be used as an example through some tough situations, then that's what will happen. You need to trust that God is still in control, regardless of how the circumstances appear.

As a Christian, single-mindedness is an important key to living in God's peace. A divided mind usually results in fear and anxiety. I don't know if your mind has ever been divided as indicated in the Bible, but mine has. *"Submit therefore to God. Resist the devil and he will flee from you. Draw near to God and He will draw near to you. Cleanse your hands, you sinners; and purify your hearts, you double-minded"* (James 4:7–8). When your mind is divided, you begin to doubt God.

Sometimes I'd tell myself, "Sure, I believe that God is in control, *but* what if He doesn't do something?" That's a divided mind. I might say that I trusted God, but I really trusted the appearance of the circumstances more than God.

To trust God means you put your faith and confidence in Him. Period! And when doubts come into your mind—because doubts often do come—you confess them, because God says He is faithful and just to forgive us of our sins and cleanse us from all unrighteousness (see 1 John 1:9). All we have to do is confess our sins, which can be as simple as doubting God.

> *"If any of you lacks wisdom, let him ask of God, who gives to all generously and without reproach, and it will be given to him. But he must ask in faith without any doubting, for the one who doubts is like the surf of the sea, driven and tossed by the wind. For that man ought not to expect that he will receive anything from the Lord, being a double-minded man, unstable in all his ways"* (James 1:5–8).

Those statements are very profound. When you ask God for anything, you must *believe*. That means you have to appropriate it as a part of your inner being and not doubt.

Those who doubt God are like the waves of the sea, blown here and there by the wind. Personally, I've found that to be absolutely true.

Peace in the Midst of Cancer

I'm going to give you a few simple principles that I have learned, and I trust they will be beneficial to you. You can refer to them from time to time and put them to use.

1. ***Don't worry.*** "Worry affects the circulation, the heart, the glands, the whole nervous system. I have never known a man who died from overwork, but many who died from doubt," said Dr. Charles Mayo. And Corrie Ten Boom said, "Worry does not empty tomorrow of its sorrow; it empties today of its strength."

   The things around you are going to become overwhelming if you're living in fear and anxiety about cancer or dying. You'll begin to have these little pity parties and you'll worry about dying, you'll decide it's not fair, and you'll begin to compare your situation to everyone else's around you.

   I know people who tell me that it was okay when they had cancer—until good friends with cancer were cured; then they found it harder to handle their own cancer. In other words, instead of rejoicing over the fact that the friends had recovered from the cancer, they felt like they had been slighted. Bad way to live.

2. **Know your strengths and weaknesses.** One of my strengths is that I'm a type "A" personality. At Crown Financial Ministries we call someone like me a "high D," or a dominant, decisive person. My strength is making decisions. I have no difficulty making decisions—good ones *and* bad ones, as a matter of fact. It is frequently said of someone with my personality, "often wrong but never in doubt." That's pretty much who I am.

I also know my weaknesses. I tend not to share personal failures with other people. It's rather unusual for me to be sharing in this manner in this book. I can do it in writing better than I can do it face-to-face, and that's a weakness. Another weakness is that I tend not to appreciate and understand the problems others are going through, because mine have to be pretty big to catch my attention. I adjust to wherever I am in life pretty quickly, and I expect others to do the same.

I've adjusted to not having a kidney and a shoulder blade and the accompanying difficulties that come with those conditions, because I'm a matter-of-fact person. (Hey, that's the way it is. Learn to live with it!) I believe God has a way of modifying our behavior in ways we might not choose. He has used my experience with cancer to make me a lot more sympathetic and empathetic toward others.

3. *Accept God's authority as absolute.* Now that's the one thing I can do. I lived 32 years as a non-believer and had nothing I believed in that was greater than me, and that's a pretty scary way to live. Now I accept God's authority as absolute. If cancer is what God has chosen or allowed for me, then that's what I accept. If God has seen in His wisdom to allow me to live in spite of the odds, and I believe He has, then I accept that as well.

There must be a reason for everything He allows in our lives. In my case I see the reason as an opportunity to lead other people to the Lord through what's happened to me. Hopefully, I also can help others who are going through problems similar to those I've experienced. I've accepted that that's why I'm still here. And God's authority is absolute.

As long as He wants me here, nothing and nobody can remove me. And when God doesn't want me here no thing nor any human being—doctor or otherwise —can keep me here. I believe that with all my heart.

4. ***Don't be angry and don't blame God.*** Anger does nothing but shorten your life expectancy, as I've already shared with you. Laughter is a healer. In fact, many times I remind myself of that when I look at things that are funny to me. For instance, I know it's a little strange, but I enjoy good commercials, and I watch them over and over again, because they make me laugh.

And while I'm laughing I'm thinking, *You know, I'm putting out some really good endorphins, because I feel good and I'm happy, and I'm doing a lot to improve my immune system.*

God didn't cause the circumstances that are happening to you. He may have allowed them, but He didn't *cause* them.

We have been given a great deal of authority in this world to make our own decisions. God said that He made us in His own image (see Genesis 1:26–30), so He's given us the ability to make our own decisions. Much of what we go through is a result of either our ignorance or our stubbornness, and I accept that. Get to know God well, because you'll be spending an eternity with Him. Don't blame God for what you go through, and don't be angry at Him.

5. *Avoid living in confusion and doubt.* American essayist Ralph Waldo Emerson said, "Knowledge is the antidote to fear." Confusion can do nothing but cause you anxiety and a lot more problems.

Settle on the best treatment you can find for you, even though it may not be the best in the world. I realize that I may not be receiving the best therapy available in the world, because I may not even know it exists. I might still have my shoulder blade if I had known at the time that a doctor at Loma Linda Medical College in California could have removed my tumor with a proton accelerator and left the scapula intact. But, at that time I didn't know it existed.

I wish I had, but I'm not going to be angry or frustrated about that. I did the best with what I knew at that time. Since then, I've expanded my research to include a greater variety of therapies. Therefore, perhaps I've avoided taking out some other part of my body that I'll probably need later on.

6. *Find the treatment that fits you and stick with it.* As important as finding a therapy that will help you is the principle of staying with it.

I talk to people all the time who continually go from one thing to another. When they hear of something else that might be good, they'll jump in that direction. As a consequence, they never complete a therapy. How will they ever know if anything helps them or not? They have done many things partially, sometimes simultaneously. They have wasted precious time and lots of money, not to speak of the discouragement and frustration they experience. In my opinion, they have divided minds—a very bad condition when you're fighting cancer. "The great thing in this world is not so much where we are, but in what direction we are moving," said Oliver Wendell Holmes.

7. *Avoid listening to too many options.* At some point, after you've gotten enough input to know what you're looking for and found what seems to be a logical therapy for you, traditional or otherwise, you need to tell your friends and family to back off. Unless they discover a miracle cure (and there aren't any), I can assure you that more input and family pressure just leads to more frustration. Even if they don't totally agree with your decision, they need to respect it.

8. *Focus on getting well.* Don't focus on "dying gracefully." I have met lots of people with cancer that I believe have focused on dying gracefully, rather than

looking for treatments that will help them stay alive and perhaps even cure them. Let me assure you, that is *not* what God wants for you. I've heard many Christians say, "I have accepted the fact that I'm going to die." There is a time when that is logical and normal, but it's not up to you to decide. Only God has that right. If you're able to read this book, it's too soon to quit.

"If [Satan] can cause you to doubt the goodness of God then there is a chance you will become fearful and give up. All God's greatest saints had to learn to handle heartaches and disappointments, along with all kinds of evil. Reading about their victories and defeats will bring insight and hope to your life."[5]

God doesn't want you to die gracefully—not unless you're sure that you have truly exhausted all the resources available to you.

9. ***Don't worry about pleasing other people all the time.*** You have a specific and designated job, and that is to get over the disease you have. Stop worrying about pleasing other people and doing what they want you to do. Do what you know is best for you and be honest about it.

By the way, that includes doctors. Don't worry about pleasing doctors. If your caregiver is doing something you don't agree with and you're afraid to speak up for fear of irritating him or her, you're absolutely wrong. It's your life. You make the decisions.

10. **Pray a lot, read a lot, and praise a lot.** This may be the most important principle of all. When you pray you talk directly to God. I know many people who know a lot *about* God, but I'm convinced they don't *know* Him. All they've done is read about God, or heard somebody talk about God, but they don't really know God in a personal way.

You know *about* God by reading or hearing about Him, but you only *know* God by talking to Him and hearing *from* Him. That means you have to pray. I believe you need to read a lot about God—especially during this crisis time in your life. And you need to have regular times to read about Him, because God will change your heart and attitudes through His Word. The better we know God's Word, the keener our spiritual senses will be. We can take our stand on God's Word and refuse to be moved.

Think about it: There's nobody you can read about in the Bible who is still alive. Even though the Lord Jesus Christ was resurrected and lives forever, He first had to die. All the characters presented in the Bible are gone. Nobody lives forever on this planet. It makes no difference how good you are, how righteous you may be, or how much you think God needs you. You're going to die. Praise God for that, because you've been allowed this time to live with your family and, if you are a believer, you're going to spend eternity with God. So praise Him a lot and don't live in self-pity. The more you praise God, the more prepared you will be to accept the next steps of His strategy for you.

11. ***Don't let money drive all your decisions.*** I've met people who make every medical decision based on whether the insurance company will pay for it. And many of these people have enough money to make their own decisions if they wanted to.

I have long since concluded that if God has given me money, and I can use it to help fight this disease, then that's probably why He gave it to me in the first place. However, don't let money drive all your decisions. It comes down to a point of trust in God.

Do you really believe and trust God, or do you just say you do? If God has directed you to a therapy that you cannot afford, then let your family and friends know. God can provide through other people.

I've observed that that's how God provides these

days—through other people. He stopped dropping manna from heaven and started using people to provide for the needs of others.

If someone is willing to help another, *"It is acceptable according to what a person has, not according to what he does not have. For this is not for the ease of others and for your affliction, but by way of equality—at this present time your abundance being a supply for their need, so that their abundance also may become a supply for your need, that there may be equality; as it is written, 'He who gathered much did not have too much, and he who gathered little had no lack'"* (2 Corinthians 8:12–15).

So, don't ever let money drive all your decisions. The bottom line is this: God wants you to be peaceful in the midst of the problems you're going through, but He does not want you to be passive. Your attitude will determine so much of how you handle life's pressures and challenges.

NOTES

1. Charles Stanley, author and pastor in Atlanta, Georgia.
2. Lloyd Ogilvie, chaplain of the U.S. Senate.
3. Brian G. Jett, author and musician.
4. William Barclay, American lawyer and politician; vice president of U.S., 1949–1953.
5. Charles Stanley, author and pastor in Atlanta, Georgia.

chapter seven
Maintaining Hope

What does hope really mean? Most cancer patients can tell you what hope means to them. Hope means that somebody will find a cure for the problems they have. Hope means that the insurance company will pay for the next procedures they need. Hope means that this disease will not infect their families.

It has been said that "True hope is inadvertent. It does not come from searching for hope. It grows out of two basic convictions: that God is in charge and that He intervenes."[1]

For me, hope means a promise for a bright future, *in spite* of the circumstances around me. The apostle Paul wrote to the church in Rome, *"In hope we have been saved, but hope that is seen is not hope; for who hopes for what he already sees?*

But if we hope for what we do not see, with perseverance we wait eagerly for it" (Romans 8:24–25).

Hope Is a Blessing

Obviously Paul was talking about salvation and heaven, but I think the principle is applicable to the situation right now as well. If you only hope for what you already have, then you really have no hope at all. For a wealthy man, hoping to be rich is foolish, because he already is rich. And it would be ridiculous for a healthy person to pray for good health when he or she already is healthy.

If you're reading this book you probably know somebody who doesn't have a lot of hope. Perhaps it's you. Perhaps you are afflicted with cancer, as I am. But you need to have hope—specifically hope that your circumstance is going to change. That doesn't mean that you hope you're going to live forever. I don't want to live forever, at least certainly not in this body. I hope they'll find a fix for the disease I have. However, there are a lot of other ways a person could die—besides from cancer—and some are more burdensome and difficult.

"Hope is necessary in every condition. The miseries of poverty, sickness, of captivity, would, without this comfort, be insupportable."[2]

Hope means knowing that others care. Christians

have been praying for my health now for about 10 years. Nothing blesses my spirit more than meeting somebody who says, "Larry, we heard about your cancer and we continue to pray for you." I tell everybody who says that, "Thank you and God bless you." I believe it's because of those prayers that I'm still here.

Our sixteenth president, Abraham Lincoln, said, "I have been driven many times to my knees, by the overwhelming conviction that I had nowhere to go but prayer. My own wisdom, and that of all about me, seemed insufficient for that day."

Hope also means knowing that God cares, and that's the most important hope of all. In spite of the circumstances, regardless of the problems we may be going through, we have to know that God is still in control.

The Psalmist said, *"Why are you in despair, O my soul? And why have you become disturbed within me? Hope in God, for I shall again praise Him for the help of His presence"* (Psalm 42:5). That's a very important attitude to maintain.

Your hope is in God. God cares about you and me and He knows exactly what we're going through. He will not let anything come upon us that will overwhelm us. As a Christian, I know that everything that is happening to me is for the advancement of the kingdom of God; and, as a result, it is therefore for my good as well.

Meet Some Hopeful Friends

I've met many people over these past few years who have had problems far worse than mine. Not only were their diseases worse, but they had progressed pretty far by the time I met them.

You see, not everyone gets well. In fact, most don't. I am not "well" myself. I still have active cancer and have simply found a way to live with it. If you live long enough, one day you'll hear about my passing. Everyone dies. Although my preferred demise is accepting the PGA super-senior, one-arm golf trophy at 100 years old and getting struck by lightning while holding it up for the cameras, dying is not the issue. Living is.

I could have chosen examples from among the patients I've known who fully recovered from their diseases, and if this were a book about the miracles I've witnessed I would have done that. But . . .

Say Hello to Martha

I'll tell you the story of a friend I'll call Martha. One day she called and explained that she had stage IV ovarian cancer. It had metastasized to her liver, colon, and lungs.

Anybody who knows anything about ovarian cancer

knows that the prognosis is seldom very good. In fact, she had gone through all the traditional treatments of chemotherapy and several experimental versions. The doctors didn't even try radiation, because the cancer was so widespread.

She had just gone through three very debilitating rounds of chemotherapy and she didn't get better; instead, she got progressively worse. During the course of the last chemotherapy treatment, she told her doctor that she had no quality of life at all and felt like she was already dead. She told him she was going to stop the chemotherapy, and she didn't want to try anything else.

The doctor said, "Well, if you do that, I won't give you three months to live."

I believe she provided the doctor with exactly the correct response. "You can't give me three months to live. God is the one who decides whether I live or die, and I don't believe I can go on living and feeling like I do now."

Martha stopped the chemotherapy, and that was when I met her. She was looking for other alternatives. She had talked to some friends who knew of my situation and that I had been taking some immune therapy in the Czech Republic, so she called me.

She was a very nice woman, with a pleasant manner and no bitterness—no "Woe is me" attitude. Martha didn't have any close family ties. Her husband had left her at the beginning of the cancer cycle, and her children were grown and had their own family responsibilities. She was pretty much trying to handle her problems on her own.

After I had several conversations with her about immune therapy, Martha went to Prague, took the immune therapy, and it worked very well for her. She wasn't cured, but she knew from the beginning that the treatment was not a cure. I had explained that the therapy was designed to help keep her immune system strong enough to fight off potential secondary diseases and perhaps even gain a degree of control over the cancer. Again, I did *not* represent this therapy as a cure for cancer and neither did anyone at the Prague clinic.

As I said, she responded very well to the therapy. And, although her cancer did not go into total remission and the tumors didn't disappear, at least their growth slowed. In fact, most of them simply stopped growing.

Martha lived for an additional three and one-half years. The difference during those years was that she had a very good quality of life (at least compared to what she had experienced while taking the chemotherapy). Almost to the final stages of her life she was active as a golfer, enjoyed herself and her friends, and had a very pleasant attitude about her life.

I really believe that God led her to me—not so I

could tell her how to survive cancer, because that's up to God, but so I could share with her what I had learned.

Martha, in turn, shared her faith in Christ with everyone she met in those last years of her life. Who knows how many people we'll see in heaven as a result of Martha's last three and one-half years?

And This Is Robert

Another person (I'll call him Robert) was also a good friend. Robert also has gone to be with the Lord.

When Robert first called me, he had been diagnosed with multiple myeloma (incurable but treatable cancer of the blood and immune system) that had spread to several locations. This is another one of those cancers that is very devastating, and his prognosis was very bad.

Robert had tried the traditional treatments but they didn't work for him. The multiple myeloma began to spread. For all intents and purposes, the doctors gave up on him and advised him to call in hospice care. If you know anything about cancer, when a doctor suggests that you request hospice care, that doctor believes you don't have very long to live.

Well, he had become familiar with my bout with cancer through Crown's radio broadcasts, and he called me. Robert had been a great supporter of Christian efforts for a long time. He was well known in his own community as the kind of person who, if you had a need, would always help.

When he contacted me, the Lord impressed on me that here was a person who was serving God, doing his very best, and needed some moral support. I realized he was probably near the end of his lifetime and at the end of his rope too. I decided that I needed to help Robert.

I asked him to come to Gainesville. We spent some time together and I helped him get started on a nutritional program. In all honesty, I had decided that anything I might suggest would at best just be soothing, but one never knows.

By the time I met Robert, the treatment from Prague had been approved in the United States, so I linked him with a doctor that was doing the therapy. Robert had a surprisingly positive physical response.

When I first met Robert, I thought he looked like the walking dead. He had just come off a series of chemotherapy treatments and had a very gray, pallid look and sunken eyes. That is not unusual for many chemotherapy patients.

However, the next time I saw Robert, about six weeks after our first meeting, he had gained about 10 pounds and his skin was pink. It was amazing. He didn't look like a specimen of good health, but he certainly looked a whole lot better than when I first saw him.

Interestingly, Robert lived almost six years beyond what the doctors had told him he would. He took no more chemotherapy or radiation and never had the need for hospice. When the Lord took Robert home, He did so suddenly, while Robert was still looking good and feeling relatively well.

I think that's what hope is all about. The lives of my friends, Martha and Robert, have served to encourage me and give me as much hope as I was able to provide them. Over the past several years I have met dozens of people like Martha and Robert—people who simply refused to give up and die.

Hope Goes Beyond

To the Christian, hope means knowing that the circumstances and the odds don't really matter, as long as we believe that God is in control. Lloyd Ogilvie says, "God is good to those who wait for Him, seek Him, and completely trust in Him. When we do that, we will be able to realistically see things as they are but also hope for what God will do."

"The grace of God has appeared, bringing salvation to all men, instructing us to deny ungodliness and worldly desires and to live sensibly, righteously and godly in the present age, looking for the blessed hope and the appearing of the glory of our great

God and Savior, Christ Jesus, who gave Himself for us to redeem us from every lawless deed, and to purify for Himself a people for His own possession, zealous for good deeds" (Titus 2:11–14).

You see, many times God speaks to us directly. At other times, God uses people and speaks through them, and I understand that. Clearly, in Robert and Martha's cases, I believe that God used me to tell them what He wanted them to hear.

Neither of them survived their cancers. They both died. However, I'm not so sure that the cancer had any greater role in their deaths than their chemotherapy may have had.

Many of my alternative medicine contacts have commented that they rarely get to see a patient until all the traditional therapies have been exhausted. That means they are left with the most difficult cases and with patients who have very depleted immune systems. This scenario won't change until the traditional and alternative are blended into complementary, not competing, therapies.

Did the alternative treatments really help? I don't know, but even placebo effects are sometimes very powerful.

I do know this: I've known many cancer patients who lived longer, had a better quality of life, and died easier than the doctors thought they could. Others are still living and doing well. And that's what hope is all about.

Hope and Faith

Hope and faith in God go together. So, if you don't believe (the word *believe* translates into "act in accordance with, or assimilate it into your spirit") in God, there is no real hope in the world, except what health professionals can do for you.

And again, when you're fighting a disease like cancer you realize pretty quickly that there's really not a lot that human beings can do for you, outside of the mercy of God. For sure, we're getting better therapies for the treatment of cancer, but we still have a very long way to go.

My question for God's people is this: Is it realistic to expect God to miraculously heal? Assume you're looking down a channel. On the right-hand side is what you think is best—that God *always* provides a miracle. On the left-hand side is what you believe is the least—that God is in control of everything but doesn't interfere in our lives. That means you may get well or may not get well, depending on "chance."

A friend I'd known for a long time got cancer. She believed in miracles to the point that, in my opinion, she boxed God in. God *had* to do a miracle for her. In other words, she believed she couldn't die from the cancer she had because it would mean God was unable to provide a miracle, and somehow that would disgrace or discredit Him.

Well, I've found that God doesn't worry about His character. Neither is He very concerned with His reputation, and He will do pretty much whatever He wants to do. Absolute authority has that right. Of course, I believe God's going to do what He promises in His Word. If God had promised in His Word that my friend was going to get over that cancer, then she would have gotten over it. However He never said that, and I tried to tell her not to put those boundaries on God. I believe that her absoluteness about miracles dissuaded her from seeking good treatments for her disease. Was that faith or presumption?

Anyone who truly believes in God knows that He is absolutely in control. I fully believe that God can perform a miracle and heal my cancer at any time. Nevertheless, up to this point, it doesn't appear that it's His sovereign will for me to be healed. Yet, I am still living.

God can use you while you are struggling with this disease just as well as if He chooses to miraculously heal you, because ultimately our purpose as believers is to bring others into the kingdom. If through what we do, how we live, even how we die, we can bring others into the kingdom, our lives will have been successful.

However, my friend was absolutely convinced that God *had* to heal her and God *was* going to heal her. She had so convinced herself of this that she refused to do any further treatment, traditional or alternative. She was determined that God was just going to supernaturally heal her.

She lived two and one-half years after being diagnosed with cancer and then died. God chose not to heal her, but He did use her. I know He used her in my life. She was a beautiful person with a sweet spirit. God also used her to convince me that you cannot tell God what to do. God makes His own decisions.

We can pray and ask God to hear us. His Word tells us to do that. We're to ask in faith believing, while keeping in mind that it is God who leads; we are to follow. *"Who are you, O man, who answers back to God? The thing molded will not say to the molder, 'Why did you make me like this,' will it?"* (Romans 9:20).

In the latter days of her life, my friend began to doubt that she was going to be healed, and then she began to doubt God because He hadn't healed her. The saddest part was that, as a result of her doubt and discouragement, she began to discourage others around her, including her own family. Doubt and discouragement destroy hope. You have to believe that God is in control, even if He doesn't do your bidding.

C.S. Lewis wrote, "Prayer is a request. The essence of request, as distinct from compulsion, is that it may or may not be granted. And if an infinitely wise Being listens to the requests of finite and foolish creatures, of course He will sometimes grant and sometimes refuse them."

I really believe that the circumstances that God allows in our lives are intended for exactly the purposes that the apostle Paul points out in writing to the church at Rome. The tribulations increase our patience, which in turn builds character, which produces hope as a result of God's love being poured into our hearts.

> "Therefore, having been justified by faith, we have peace with God through our Lord Jesus Christ, through whom also we have obtained our introduction by faith into this grace in which we stand; and we exult in hope of the glory of God. And not only this, but we also exult in our tribulations, knowing that tribulation brings about perseverance; and perseverance, proven character; and proven character, hope; and hope does not disappoint, because the love of God has been poured out within our hearts through the Holy Spirit who was given to us" (Romans 5:1–5).

Be sure that your faith and hope is based on the reality of the truth of God's Word and not simply on some wished-for dream.

Keep On Being Happy and Hopeful

Harvey Mindess, psychologist and psychoanalyst, said, "Pointing out the comic elements of a situation can bring a sense of proportion and perspective to what might otherwise seem an overwhelming problem."

Learn to laugh. Laugh a lot with other people and learn to laugh at yourself as well.

Personally, I really like corny movies. I have taken a few scenes from a couple of my favorite movies and recorded them. If you want to see what is arguably the stupidest movie ever produced, watch *Mars Attack.* That qualifies as my choice for number one wackiest movie ever produced—and I love it.

Another favorite is *Monty Python and the Holy Grail.* Now, this one has some scenes you won't want your children or grandchildren to watch, but it is very funny. The *Pink Panther* movies are some of my favorites too. I know that Peter Sellers wasn't the nicest guy in the world, but he was a funny actor.

"Guard well your spare moments. They are like uncut diamonds. Discard them and their value will never be known. Improve them and they will become the brightest gems in a useful life."[3] God wants you to enjoy yourself. Focus on living your life, not dying.

I had a good friend who died of renal cell carcinoma —the same disease I have. He was diagnosed about a year before I was and died within three years; but he never lost his sense of humor. He was always praising God and leading a Bible study. Because he couldn't get out, members of his Bible study class came to his home. Until the day he died he was happy and a very positive person who was a joy to be around. I consider it a great honor and privilege to be one of his friends, and I look forward to seeing him again one day.

The apostle Paul's advice to the church at Philippi was pretty sound: *"Whatever is true, whatever is honorable, whatever is right, whatever is pure, whatever is lovely, whatever is of good repute, if there is any excellence and if anything worthy of praise, dwell on these things. The things you have learned and received and heard and seen in me, practice these things, and the God of peace will be with you"* (Philippians 4:8–9).

Concentrate On Living

Concentrate on living—not on dying. Focus on positive things instead of the negatives. I don't have a right kidney and my right side hurts—a lot! I don't have a left shoulder blade and my left shoulder hurts—a whole lot! However, I refuse to give in to pain and to focus on the negative things I can't do; and there are a lot of things I can't do.

For example, I can't work on old cars any more, which I used to enjoy very much. I've sold all my old cars. I can't do lawn work anymore, but I used to hate yard work, so that's a good thing. I can't lift my left arm above my waist since I had my scapula removed, so I don't paint anymore unless it's below my waist—that's not bad either.

You see, if you focus on the things you can't do,

you'll never accomplish anything. So focus on the things you can do. You know what you can do? You can have fun with your family. You can love them and care for them.

One of my grandsons and I go fishing and we go to Dollywood and go on the rides. I play golf, even though I don't play very well. My brother says, "It's okay that you don't play very well now, because you didn't play all that well before either!" Regardless of his opinion of my game, I enjoy it because it's a good time to get out in the fresh air with friends.

I'm taking pleasure in doing this particular book, because I enjoy writing. There are lots of things I can focus on that are positive, without having to focus on the negatives. And I also believe that you can live longer and have much more hope if you are positive.

Good Things Ahead

Let me offer some other things to give you hope. I really think that traditional medicine and alternative medicine both are very close to some major cancer breakthroughs. The genetic research that is seeking to engineer a cure for cancer will happen sometime in the very near future, probably within this decade. For millions of us, that's going to represent as close to a cure as we may ever see.

We are going to see vaccines made that will control tumors, and I believe that eventually we will have vaccines for the majority of cancers that afflict us. Thus, we will have the potential to keep most people from ever getting cancer. We'll find the genetic defects that make cancers prevalent with some families and correct those defects. I absolutely believe that we're very far along with much of this exciting research.

If we could stop fighting wars and direct some of that money to cancer research, perhaps we could virtually eradicate most cancers in the next 20 years.

Do you think that sounds far-fetched? I remember when President Kennedy announced we would land a man on the moon and bring him back safely in the decade of the 1960s. We've sent 10 there and back.

When God designed us, He gave us His intelligence. We have the ability to maintain these bodies at very high levels, and that's a very positive thing. In my case, even though they haven't discovered a cure for my cancer, I have found treatments that have kept me alive until now and might continue to do so until somebody finds a cure or I die from something else.

Accentuate the Positive

Overall, hope means maintaining a positive attitude. Popular songwriter Johnny Mercer wrote music of unusual quality and imagery from 1930 until his death from a brain tumor in 1976. Legend has it that in the mid-1940s, while he was driving home from a psychiatric session, he decided to take his doctor's suggestion to "accentuate the positive," and he turned the advice into a song. One of the lines went something like this: "You've gotta accentuate the positive, eliminate the negative, latch on to the affirmative, and don't mess with mister in-between." That's good counsel.

While you or a loved one are going through a difficult time, do the things that will help you maintain a positive attitude. Stop being negative. Negativity does not come from God. Besides, your negativity not only gets you down, it will also depress everybody around you, depress your immune system, and ultimately kill you.

I don't know what you might want to do in order to remain positive, but I do lots of things. I love the History Channel on TV, so whenever I can't sleep at night I watch history. I love biographies, so I read real-life stories of great people. Incidentally, one of the things I've noticed is that almost all of the biographies I'm reading are of people who have died. I take that as good evidence that you can die and still have accomplished a great deal with your life.

In fact, it's a guarantee that if the Lord doesn't come first we're all going to die. That's not a negative. That's a positive. Maintain hope in your life and don't give up. Believe that God is in control, love your family and your friends, be a positive influence for the Lord, and lead others to the Lord. After all, when we leave this world, the only thing that will go with us will be the people who have followed Jesus Christ. And that hope has been guaranteed for God's children in His Word.

> *"God, desiring even more to show to the heirs of the promise the unchangeableness of His purpose, interposed with an oath, so that by two unchangeable things in which it is impossible for God to lie, we who have taken refuge would have strong encouragement to take hold of the hope set before us. This hope we have as an anchor of the soul, a hope both sure and steadfast and one which enters within the veil, where Jesus has entered as a forerunner for us, having become a high priest forever according to the order of Melchizedek"* (Hebrews 6:17–20).

"God knows what you need. Don't give up and try to satisfy that need your own way. Wait on Him, and He will take care of you according to His goodness."[4] Maintain the hope that God has implanted in your heart through the Holy Spirit, because it is a sure and steadfast hope that will serve you well as a solid anchor for your soul. That's what I call accentuating the positive.

NOTES

1. Lloyd Ogilvie, chaplain of the U.S. Senate.
2. Samuel Johnson, lexicographer and author.
3. Ralph Waldo Emerson, American essayist and poet (1803–1882).
4. Charles Stanley, author and pastor in Atlanta, Georgia.

chapter eight
Wisdom

As anybody who suffers with cancer can tell you, one thing we all need during this time is *wisdom.* My definition of wisdom is *knowledge in action.* Or perhaps another way to characterize wisdom is that it is useable knowledge.

There are a lot of people who have knowledge that's not useable to others, because they can't explain it or apply it. I have found that true of many professionals—engineers and scientists—and I've certainly found it true of some doctors. One of my college professors used to say, "Most people answer questions that nobody asks. A wise person answers the questions that others ask."

Many people with important information have never learned to apply knowledge in action to help other people. Why? Because it is God who gives us wisdom. In God's Word we're told, *"For the Lord gives wisdom; from His mouth come knowledge and understanding"* (Proverbs 2:6). It's very important to remember that "wisdom is the mind of God implanted in the tissues of our brains. It is God's thought controlling our thought. It results in an immense discernment and knowledge beyond our own human capacity."[1]

Another principle to remember is found in God's Word: *"If any of you lacks wisdom, let him ask of God, who gives to all generously and without reproach, and it will be given to him"* (James 1:5).

Let me assure you, I have applied that principle many times in my life, before and since I've had cancer. If you lack wisdom, you only have to *"ask of God."* He gives generously and without finding fault.

Faith, Prayer, and You

It goes without saying that Christians are to be in continual communication with God. When you get in a situation with multiple options and you really don't know what you should do, pray. God promises that if you ask in faith, believing, He will provide for you. *"The prayer of the upright is His delight"* (Proverbs 15:8).

Richard Chenevix Trench wrote, "Prayer is not overcoming God's reluctance; it is laying hold of His highest willingness."[2] The essence of wisdom is both faith and prayer; in other words, believe and ask.

So, don't be bashful about asking God. His Word says to *"draw near with confidence to the throne of grace, so that we may receive mercy and find grace to help in time of need"* (Hebrews 4:16).

Let me give an example. I mentioned earlier that when I was first diagnosed with my shoulder problem I went to several orthopedists. Every one of them misdiagnosed my problem. One said it was bursitis, another diagnosed it as a rotator cuff tear, and still another said it was arthritis. The last orthopedist I saw was absolutely convinced he knew what the problem was. He wanted to do orthoscopic surgery on my left shoulder to trim some of the small bone that goes under the collarbone. He was convinced that would fix the problem. He was a nice guy and very persuasive.

We actually scheduled the surgery for about three weeks from the time I last saw him. I committed to pray about it, just to be sure I had God's wisdom and peace. However, I didn't. In fact, I didn't have any peace about it at all; and, the closer we got to the time for surgery the less peace I had and the more confused I was. I thought I was holding to my commitment to seek God's wisdom and His peace, but I wasn't absolutely sure that I wasn't just trying to avoid the surgery (ever feel that way?).

I called him about three or four days before the scheduled surgery and told him I'd like to cancel. He was quite irritated about it and asked why I had changed my mind. I told him that I wasn't sure—I just didn't have peace about his diagnosis. (Try that one on your average doctor.)

He sarcastically challenged my "diagnosis" and wanted to know what I thought the problem was. I had to admit that I didn't know. And that was the honest truth: I didn't have a clue. All I had to go on was a feeling. I just felt like it wasn't the problem he had diagnosed. Well, of course, he was very upset and our conversation ended. I would have had a hard time getting another appointment with him at that time.

It was a short time later that I called my friend at Emory and went over to the Emory Sports Clinic in Atlanta. I went through the diagnostic clinic and they determined that the problem was *not* in my shoulder. Ultimately the doctor there was the one who called for an MRI, which correctly diagnosed it as a tumor under my shoulder blade.

If I had gone through with the surgery, not only would it have not helped the pain, it would have delayed the appropriate diagnosis. Perhaps it would have caused other complications, and who knows if I'd still be here.

I believe the wisdom to refuse the procedure that was proposed by the orthopedic surgeon came directly from the

Lord. God simply provided the wisdom I needed when I needed it (see Proverbs 12:15).

Wisdom and You

I believe there are three essential elements to finding wisdom.

- **_Personal faith in Jesus Christ._** When the woman who had been hemorrhaging came up to Jesus and touched Him, she believed that Jesus was going to heal her. The Scriptures indicate that Jesus didn't know her; nor did she know Him, except by observation. She didn't know the plan of salvation at the time, and we aren't even certain that she was a Jew.

  > _"A woman who had a hemorrhage for twelve years, and could not be healed by anyone, came up behind [Jesus] and touched the fringe of His cloak, and immediately her hemorrhage stopped. . . . Jesus said, 'Someone did touch Me, for I was aware that power had gone out of Me.' When the woman saw that she had not escaped notice, she came trembling and fell down before Him, and declared in the presence of all the people the reason why she had touched Him, and how she had been immediately healed. And He_

said to her, 'Daughter, your faith has made you well; go in peace'" (Luke 8:43–48).

This woman had a personal belief that Jesus could help her—enough that she was willing to walk through a crowd and touch the hem of His garment, knowing that if she did He would heal her. She simply *believed* that Jesus *could* heal her and that He *would* heal her. That's personal faith in Jesus Christ.

If that same woman had lived in the 1960s, she might have heard the late Dr. Martin Luther King, Jr. say, "Take the first step in faith. You don't have to see the whole staircase, just take the first step."

- *Faith of others.* Because there are times when our faith may be a bit lacking, we may need the faith of our friends. I believe that often, when my faith was wavering, there were friends who carried me through that period by praying for me, even when I couldn't pray for myself.

  Dwight L. Moody was fond of pointing out that there are three kinds of faith in Jesus Christ: *struggling* faith, which is like a man floundering and fearful in deep water; *clinging* faith, which is like a man hanging to the side of a boat; and *resting* faith, which finds a man safe inside the boat—strong and secure enough to reach out his hand to help someone else.

I think the biblical account of the friends of the paralytic man is a good illustration of this principle. Jesus was teaching in a home and it was so crowded that no one else could get into the building. Fortunately, this paralyzed man had four friends who were determined that he was going to see Jesus.

> "They came, bringing to [Jesus] a paralytic, carried by four men. Being unable to get to Him because of the crowd, they removed the roof above Him; and when they had dug an opening, they let down the pallet on which the paralytic was lying. And Jesus seeing their faith said to the paralytic, 'Son, your sins are forgiven'" (Mark 2:3–5).

There were some Jewish scholars there who were offended, and they accused Jesus of blasphemy for saying such a thing. They knew only God could forgive sin. Then Jesus said to those scribes,

> "Why are you reasoning about these things in your hearts? Which is easier, to say to the paralytic, 'Your sins are forgiven'; or to say, 'Get up, and pick up your pallet and walk'? But so that you may know that the Son of Man has

*authority on earth to forgive sins—He said to the paralytic,
'I say to you, get up, pick up your pallet and go home.' And
he got up and immediately picked up the pallet and went
out in the sight of everyone, so that they were all amazed
and were glorifying God, saying, 'We have never seen anything like this'"* (Mark 2:8–12).

The paralytic man *might* have believed, but the
Word doesn't say he did. However, because of the de-
termination and faith of his friends, Jesus healed him.

- **Persistence.** The Scripture clearly indicates that God
  appreciates those who are persistent. A great example
  of this is the widow who came to a judge's door in the
  middle of the night to get legal protection from an op-
  ponent. Apparently, this judge wasn't a very nice guy. The
  Bible says that the judge did not fear God or respect
  man and, not wanting to be bothered, he kept telling
  the widow to go away.

  Nevertheless, she continued to bang on his door;
  and she was so persistent that finally he got up and said,
  *"I will give her legal protection, otherwise by continually
  coming she will wear me out"* (Luke 18:5).

  To make His point, Jesus said that if an unrigh-
  teous judge would do that, *"Will not God bring about*

justice for His elect who cry to Him day and night, and will He delay long over them?" (Luke 18:7).

This story illustrates that through persistence the widow received what she needed. There are many examples similar to this in Scripture demonstrating the principle of persistence. *"So I say to you, ask, and it will be given to you; seek, and you will find; knock, and it will be opened to you. For everyone who asks, receives; and he who seeks, finds; and to him who knocks, it will be opened"* (Luke 11:9–10).

Persistence is one of the characteristics of a faithful steward who needs and wants God's wisdom. To get through the hardest journey, we need to take only one step at a time, but we must keep on stepping. Be like the persistent widow who needed justice. Don't give up. And if you don't receive God's answer the first time you ask, keep on asking.

Know Your Body

It is very important that you are in tune with your body, because aside from God no one really knows more about what's going on inside your body than you do. Pay attention to what's going on, and take care of your body. It's the only one you'll have this side of heaven.

Let me explain to you why I think it's so important

for you to know your own body. Each of us is different from everyone else in the world. For example, I am very close to my older brother. In many ways we are quite similar: We have the same parents, were raised in the same home, had basically the same background and environment, and yet we are two totally different people.

When I was on a tear to lower my cholesterol, I found that using niacin and a high-fiber diet lowered my cholesterol significantly. I told my brother about it, and he got on the same diet; but it didn't help him at all. Yet we came from the same parents, background, and so forth.

On another occasion, he was taking a blood pressure medicine that was really effective for him and he told me about it. I asked my doctor to prescribe some for me so I could see how it would work. I tried it, and it didn't work for me. We are all different. The treatment that works for one person may or may not work for someone else. So, know your own body.

Regarding your pursuit of a cure, learn to trust your instincts. Quite often, when a Christian thinks that his or her instincts are speaking, it is the Holy Spirit giving His guidance.

It needs to be repeated that hucksters abound in medical treatments, both in the alternative and the traditional sense. I have met many well-meaning people who gave terrible medical advice. Some were just promoting some product or treatment and preying on the gullible. Others were honest but misled. Either way, they could kill you with bad advice, so you need to learn to trust your instincts. Of course, you also need to exercise wisdom—knowledge in action—when it comes to your treatment.

Nutrition and You

Another imperative for applying wisdom in the area of cancer is to practice good nutrition, and I'm talking about good nutrition *in balance*. That means you should keep your diet reasonable, make it fit your lifestyle, and stick with it.

As I shared with you earlier, there are some things that I can do and some that I can't. I can change the water I drink. It's not that much of an effort to buy filtered and ozonated water, so I do that. I can stop eating junk food and I did (well, almost). I can stop eating red meat and chicken, so I did.

There are lots of relatively simple things that I can do. Fundamentally, I maintain a good diet. It is not a perfect diet by any means. In fact, a nutritionist might follow me around and say, "Oh, my goodness, is that what you eat? Your diet is terrible. You don't eat all the proper things." Of course I know that raw organic vegetables and glacier water might be better for me, but based on my lifestyle that doesn't seem possible.

Therefore, I'm on the best nutritional plan that I can manage and still balance my lifestyle.

Active and Alert

Another key element involved with wisdom is to stay active and alert. Keep a good attitude. The more inward thinking you are, the more likely you are to get ill and the sooner you might die.

The more active you are, the more likely you are to stay healthy. I'm convinced that our bodies were made to wear out gradually; they were not made to get sick and die. I honestly believe that our bodies could function for 100 years or more if kept in good health.

Attitude and activity are essential. Yes, I have cancer, but I'm not about to curl up in a corner and give up living. Muscles atrophy if you don't use them and your brain will too if you don't use it. So stay active spiritually, physically, and mentally.

Don't Button up Your Brain

The next principle is to be open to new ideas. However, at the same time you need to be discerning about them. Don't be closed-minded, because if you are you might skip over treatments that have the potential to effectively fight your disease.

But be discerning. Decide ahead of time the criteria you will use to evaluate a new therapy. By that I mean you should predetermine *your own* standards for how you're going to evaluate a treatment. In Chapter Five I gave you the criteria I use.

Way Above Average

Bear in mind that our health system works on averages, and you may not be an average person. In fact, if you're reading this book, my guess is that you probably don't fit the definition of the *average* cancer patient. Perhaps your cancer hasn't been cured through the traditional methods, and now you're going to have to look outside the system.

You don't have to consider alternatives treatments; many people don't, and they get well. However, if you don't, simply because you allow your choices to be blocked by the stigma that traditional medicine attaches to alternative medicine, you might pass up a treatment that could help you.

Stay Focused

Another principle for you to remember is to focus on staying alive and well. That's what I'm trying to do.

I feel fine, usually. There's no question that I have some limitations, but I try to focus on the abilities I still have, rather than on the limitations. These bodies God has designed for us are truly remarkable. They can take an incredible amount of punishment, junk foods, pollutants, and diseases—and still recover.

Our bodies are very much like the slogan that Timex once used in their commercials for advertising the reliability of their watches: "They take a lickin' and keep on tickin'." And that's what God wants for you: to keep on ticking. So, focus on staying alive and well. You still have a whole lot of "ticking" to do.

God Above All

"Much that worries us beforehand can afterward, quite unexpectedly, have a happy and simple solution. Worries just don't matter. Things really are in a better hand than ours," said Dietrich Bonhoeffer.

Above all else, trust *in* the Lord, and *trust* the Lord. He cares about you, and He loves you more than anyone else does—more than your own mother, your father, or your children. Many years ago, Andrae Crouch, a musician who truly loves the Lord, wrote a song that says, "Through it all, through it all, I've learned to trust in God." Let that be your song.

God cares about what's going on in your life. Pray for Him to intervene on your behalf. And get your friends to pray for you too. You may not need to be lowered down through the roof for healing like the paralyzed man in the Bible, but no one can have too many friends praying for him or her. Martin Luther said, "None can believe how powerful prayer is . . . but those who have learned it by experience."

As I have said many times, nobody lives forever in these bodies, and unless the Lord Jesus Christ returns first we will all die. But God told us that a seed can't grow into a plant or a tree until it first dies. Therefore, when we pass from this life we will pass on to a more excellent and expanded life, as we enter eternity with our Lord Jesus Christ, creator of this universe (see John 1:1–5 and Genesis 1:1–31).

I pray that this book has been some small help to those who are suffering from this horrible disease called cancer.

And to the loved ones of those who suffer, remember that you have a wonderful opportunity and a great responsibility to support the person you love who has this disease. Don't let him or her wallow in self-pity, and don't you wallow in it either. Together, live your lives to the fullest in Jesus Christ.

Accept what you have and go on from there. Don't grieve over what you used to have or what you wish you had. Instead, live your life to the fullest with the circumstances you do have. I sincerely believe that God still has great plans in store for you. Today truly *is* just the beginning of the rest of your life.

Be comforted and reassured by what God's Word says, *"I will never desert you, nor will I ever forsake you"* (Hebrews 13:5). Then you can *"confidently say, 'The Lord is my helper, I will not be afraid'"* (Hebrews 13:6). "Our weapons are the Word of God and prayer and our protection is the complete armor."[3]

NOTES

1. Lloyd Ogilvie, chaplain of the U.S. Senate.
2. From *God's Best for Your Life,* Lloyd Ogilvie.
3. Warren W. Wiersbe, international Bible conference teacher and author.

Appendix

This data is provided only as information and is not intended as endorsements of advice, counsel, medical diagnoses, or treatments. We encourage you to be certain that any resource you choose is compatible with your own convictions and needs. Always consult your primary health care provider about any of your personal health concerns.

Books

Beating Cancer with Nutrition, Patrick Quillin with Noreen Quillin (Nutrition Times Press, Inc.: Tulsa, Oklahoma).

Betrayal of Health: The Impact of Nutrition, Environment, and Lifestyle on Illness in America, Joseph Beasley (Random House: New York).

Bible Cure, The, Reginald Cherry, M.D. (Creation House: Lake Mary, Florida).

Cancer Battle Plan and Healthy Habits, The, David and Anne Frahm (Piñon Press: Colorado Springs, Colorado).

Energy Edge, The, Pamela Smith, R.D. (Lifeline Press: Washington, D.C.).

Food and Love, Dr. Gary Smalley (Tyndale House Publishers: Wheaton, Illinois).

Food for Life, Pamela Smith, R.D. (Creation House: Lake Mary, Florida).

Foods That Heal, Maureen Solomon (Statford Publishing: Menlo Park, Calfornia).

God's Way to Ultimate Health, Dr. George Malkmus with Michael Dye (Hallelujah Acres Publishing: Shelby, North Carolina).

Hope When It Hurts (formerly titled *Damaged But Not Broken*), Larry Burkett with Michael E. Taylor (Moody Press: Chicago, Illinois).

I Don't Remember Signing Up for Cancer, Sherry Karuza Waldrip (WinePress Publishing: Mukilteo, Washington).

Intuitive Eating, Humbart Santillo, M.D. (Holm Press: Prescott, Arizona).

Liver Cleansing Diet, Sandra Cabot, M.D. (SCB International: Scottsdale, Arizona).

Prostate Cancer: What I Found Out and What You Should Know, Robert L. Maddox (Harold Shaw Publishers: Wheaton, Illinois).

Reclaim Your Health, David and Anne Frahm (Piñon Press: Colorado Springs, Colorado).

Toxic Terror: The Truth Behind the Cancer Scares, Elizabeth Whelan (Prometheus Books: Buffalo, New York).

Water Fit to Drink, Carol Keough (Rodale Press: Emmaus, Pennsylvania).

What the Bible Says About Healthy Living: Three Biblical Principles That Will Change Your Diet and Improve Your Health Rex Russell, M.D. (Regal Books: Ventura, California). Available in several languages (see http://www.bsahealthyliving.com).

When Cancer Comes: Mobilizing Physical, Emotional, and Spiritual Resources to Combat One of Life's Most Dreaded Diseases, Don Hawkins, Daniel L. Koppersmith, Ginger

Koppersmith (Moody Press: Chicago, Illinois). (Out of print; check your local library.)

Winning the Fight Against Breast Cancer: The Nutritional Approach, Carlton Fredericks (Grosset & Dunlap: New York).

You Don't Have to Die, Harry M. Hoxsey (Milestone Books: New York). Out of print, check local libraries.

Your Body, God's Temple, Ronald L. Kleyn, M.D. (Essence Publishing: Ontario, Canada).

Internet Search Engines

Google **http://www.google.com** Larry's personal favorite. Especially helpful in finding good sites in response to general searches such as "alternative medicine" and "cancer."

Lycos **http://www.hotbot.lycos.com**

Northern Light **http://www.northernlight.com** Variety of helpful sub-search links.

Teoma **http://www.teoma.com** Relevancy decided by ranking sites based on the number of same-subject pages that reference it as an authority.

Yahoo **http://www.yahoo.com**

Internet Sites

http://www.about.com See "search engine basics for beginners." The *about.com* site has a variety of helpful links, but be aware that many links are little more than product infomercials.

http://www.about.com/health/ Again, some links are infomercials for products.

http://www.am2treatment.com Biorem, Inc. provides the immuno-modulating treatments in the United States that were developed at the Aliatros Medical research group in the Czech Republic.

http://www.bsahealthyliving.com Healthy Living Ministries, Inc. teaches principles of health that are biblically based and scientifically sound.

http://www.cancer.gov The National Cancer Institute Web site contains helpful information and free publications to order online, or call toll free at (800) 4-CANCER.

http://www.cdc.gov The U.S. Department of Health and Human Services Web site of the Centers for Disease Control and Prevention.

http://www.crown.org/cancerinfo General information about Larry's recent cancer treatments, cryoablation and radiofrequency ablation, and cancer-related articles.

http://www.healthfinder.gov Government health information referral service. Does not diagnose medical conditions, offer medical advice, or endorse specific products or services.

http://www.medhelp.org National Library of Medicine site provides access to over 11 million citations, plus life science journals and links to sites with full text articles.

http://www.sciencekomm.at Largest online medical and science reference site.

http://www.umc.edu The University of Mississippi Medical Center.

http://www.usnews.com The 2001 *U.S. News & World Report* ranked America's hospitals according to 17 specialties. The top ten hospitals specializing in cancer are as follows:

Memorial Sloan-Kettering Cancer Center, New York
http://www.mskcc.org.
University of Texas, M.D. Anderson Cancer Center, Houston
http://www.cancerwise.org

Johns Hopkins Hospital, Baltimore
http://www.hopkinsmedicine.org/hopkinshospital
Dana-Farber Cancer Institute, Boston
http://www.dana-farber.net
Mayo Clinic, Rochester, Minnesota
http://www.mayoclinic.org
UCLA Medical Center, Los Angeles
http://www.healthcare.ucla.edu/default.htm
University of Chicago Hospitals
http://www.uchospitals.edu
Duke University Medical Center, Durham, North Carolina
http://www.cancer.duke.edu
Hospital of the University of Pennsylvania, Philadelphia
http://www.oncolink.com
Stanford University Hospital, Stanford, California
http://www-med.stanford.edu/school/oncology

http://www.worldimage.com/amd.html *Alternative Medicine Digest,* 1-800-818-6777.

Other

Georgia SB341 was passed during the 1997 Georgia State Legislative session. This law gives individuals the right to be treated by a person licensed to practice medicine with medical treatments desired or authorized under the conditions specified in the law.

Coenzyme Q-10 As an antioxidant, Coenzyme Q-10 acts to prevent cellular damage caused by unstable (free radical) oxygen molecules.

https://www.juiceplus.com Juice Plus+®. Available in both fruit and vegetable supplements.

http://www.crown.org/tools/Personality.asp Crown Financial Ministries' *Personality I.D.* is a free interactive on-line tool that will help you view others and yourself from a fresh perspective.

Acknowledgments

I would like to thank Greg Thornton and Bill Thrasher of Moody Publishers for their inspiration and encouragement to write this book.

Also, I would like to thank Dr. Harvey Nowland for his help in piecing my thoughts together.

And I thank Adeline Griffith, the best editor in Christendom.

Larry Burkett

About the Author

LARRY BURKETT was a well-known authority on business and personal finance, and wrote more than seventy books, including nonfiction best-sellers like *The Family Financial Workbook, Debt-Free Living,* and *The World's Easiest Guide to Finances.* His four radio programs were carried on more than 2,000 radio outlets worldwide. Larry founded Christian Financial Concepts in 1976, a ministry dedicated to teaching biblical principles of handling money. CFC merged with Crown Ministries in September 2000 to form Crown Financial Ministries, with Larry as chairman of the board of directors. Larry is survived by his wife, Judy, and their four grown children: Allen, Kimberly, Danny, and Todd and nine granchildren.

SINCE 1894, Moody Publishers has been dedicated to equip and motivate people to advance the cause of Christ by publishing evangelical Christian literature and other media for all ages, around the world. Because we are a ministry of the Moody Bible Institute of Chicago, a portion of the proceeds from the sale of this book go to train the next generation of Christian leaders.

If we may serve you in any way in your spiritual journey toward understanding Christ and the Christian life, please contact us at www.moodypublishers.com.

"All Scripture is God-breathed and is useful for teaching, rebuking, correcting and training in righteousness, so that the man of God may be thoroughly equipped for every good work."
—*2 TIMOTHY 3:16, 17*

MOODY
PUBLISHERS

THE NAME YOU CAN TRUST®

NOTHING TO FEAR TEAM

ACQUIRING EDITOR
Greg Thornton

COPY EDITOR
Adeline Griffith

BACK COVER COPY
Julie-Allyson Ieron, Joy Media

COVER DESIGN
Smartt Guys

COVER PHOTO
David P. Hall/Masterfile

INTERIOR DESIGN
Ragont Design

PRINTING AND BINDING
Versa Press, Inc.

The typeface for the text of this book is
Berkeley